PENTECOSTAL RAYS
The Baptism and Gifts of the Holy Spirit

Principal George Jeffreys

GEORGE JEFFREYS

This work is in the Public Domain and has been re-released as part of the Kairos Revival Classic Series.

Editor's Introduction.

'Pentecostal Rays' is a rare Pentecostal classic, and it is my joy, as the Series Editor of Kairos Revival Classics, to present this new edition to a new generation of readers. Its author, Principal George Jeffreys, has been described as, "one of the greatest evangelists that England has produced, after George Whitfield and John Wesley."

Jeffreys was a British Pentecostal pioneer, an evangelist, a pastor, a church planter, and a man who moved in signs and wonders.

'Pentecostal Rays' captures the theology of the early Pentecostal movement. It also captures the depth, and breadth of the knowledge of the author. Jeffreys handles scripture and history with a skillful hand. This book is a must-read for students of Pentecostal history, however it is also of great value for all Christians as it points the reader to a deeper relationship with the Holy Spirit.

Whilst this book is of tremendous historical interest and spiritual value, the reader should read some sections with caution.

In the early days, Pentecostal theology was still being worked out. Sometimes the early Pentecostals expressed their views in ways that could be regarded as unorthodox. One of the examples of this is Chapter 4, where Jeffreys distinguishes between the Spirit of Christ and the Holy Spirit. Jeffreys distinguishes these terms in a way that is not scriptural. For example, Jeffreys says: "God's great gift to the unregenerate is the Spirit of Christ. God's great gift to the regenerate is the Holy Spirit." On the surface level, this teaching could be labelled as heretical. However, I don't think Jeffreys was a heretic, I think he was just clumsy in this instance. Jeffreys was aiming to distinguish between the work of the Spirit in regeneration, and the work of the Spirit in empowering the regenerate believer for service. Many of the early Pentecostals were not academic theologians, they were ordinary believers who experienced the power of God and were seeking to work this experience out Biblically.

As a Pastor and teacher, who is responsible for editing and re-releasing this edition, I feel it is important to highlight this error in Jeffrey's work. This is in no way intended to take anything away from Jeffreys. The best of men are men at best. And while we can glean so much from reading the works of these spiritual giants, it is important that we test all teachings against the scriptures.

I pray this book blesses you and leads you into a greater experience of the Holy Spirit.

>   John Caldwell, Editor.
>   www.john-caldwell.com
>   www.kairoschurch.co.uk

Contents.

Foreword.

Chapter I. The Day Of Pentecost.

Chapter II. The Great Outpouring.

Chapter III. The Holy Spirit Personality—Terms—Views.

Chapter IV. The Spirit Of Christ And The Holy Spirit.

Chapter V. More Than Twenty Years After Pentecost.

Chapter VI. Three Baptisms Of The New Testament.

Chapter VII. Three Baptisms In Type.

Chapter VIII. The Relations Of The Holy Spirit To

Chapter IX. Fruit Of The Spirit And The Gifts Of The Holy Spirit.

Chapter X. The Gift Of Tongues.

Chapter XI. The Utility Of Speaking In Tongues.

Chapter XII. The Gift Of Prophecy.

Chapter XIII. Miraculous Gifts In Evidence Throughout The Present Age.

Chapter XIV. Baptism In The Holy Spirit.

Chapter XV. The Supernatural In The Local Church. Chapter XVI. Conclusion.

Foreword.

by one who has witnessed the phenomena of Pentecost under the Author's ministry.

The twentieth century Church has experienced a miraculous manifestation of the Holy Spirit's power unparalleled in her history since the first few centuries of the Christian era. A revival of the supernatural gifts of the Holy Spirit is in evidence. The outbreak of revival was spontaneous and not organised, breaking forth in different parts, and among different groups of Christians at the same time. The great opportunity for evangelical churches had arrived. At their disposal was power adequate to combat materialism and spiritism. But they did not know the day of their visitation.

In consequence of the Church's official attitude, which was Pharisaical, numbers of Christians found themselves virtually excommunicated, and generally met together in back-street mission halls and in private houses. The result was that Pentecost went back to the upper room and stayed there, except for a few urgent souls who became foreign missionaries.

Such was the condition that obtained in the British Isles when the author of this book was guided by the Holy Spirit to found the Elim Foursquare Gospel Alliance. Against fanatical opposition from sincere but mistaken people from within, and organised prejudice from without, Principal George Jeffreys led the movement to the public, and established its churches in main thoroughfares of each of the four countries of the British Isles, besides sending missionaries to different parts of the world.

On the nineteenth centenary of Pentecost the largest hall in the provinces of England was packed for the conclusion of a campaign in that city through which ten thousand people were converted.

For eight years the Royal Albert Hall, London, has been crowded at the annual Easter Convention, and at Whitsuntide meetings in the same hall about three hundred received "the Holy Spirit, with supernatural signs, in one day.

Every national newspaper has carried the news of the Principal's phenomenal success in his revival and healing campaigns. No man living is more qualified to speak with authority on this subject. Behind every sentence is twenty years of singular experience. From a wide field of historical research evidence has been deduced to prove the continuity of the supernatural gifts, and that they were not early withdrawn, as generally supposed. Not only is the case presented, we believe beyond controversy, for the miraculous signs and gifts of the Holy Spirit to-day, but to those who have been extreme in the use of the gifts, and have over-emphasised the speaking in tongues, this work presents a challenge. It tells what the gift of tongues is for, and what it is not for. Also it explains the purposes of the gifts of the Holy Spirit, how, when, and where they are to be used. To every open-minded Christian it will be evident that any system of worship without these gifts is incomplete.

James McWhirter.

GEORGE JEFFREYS

Pentecostal Rays.

Pentecostal Rays! Yes, rays of light from the Inspired Word upon a subject that is claiming the attention of the Christian Church universally—the baptism of the Holy Spirit and miraculous gifts. A baptism received in the first century by one hundred and twenty believers in the ancient city of Jerusalem, some seven weeks after the resurrection of Christ, is now received by tens of thousands of believers in the twentieth century all over the world, in view of the Second Advent of Christ. The miraculous gifts so conspicuous in the Early Church during the first few centuries are finding their place to a greater degree in the closing days of the dispensation. The gates of worldliness, unbelief, opposition, and compromise, which resulted in the gifts practically ceasing, are giving way before the onward march of an empowered Church. This companion book to "Healing Rays" simply contains the subject matter of our studies and addresses given during eighteen years' ministry amongst those who have earnestly contended for the faith, put into literary form in response to the increasing requests of succeeding years.

Chapter 1. The Day Of Pentecost.

Scenes and Circumstances Prior to the Outpouring

And when He was come near, He beheld the city, and wept over it, saying, If thou hadst known, even thou, at least in this thy day, the things which belong unto thy peace! but now they are hid from thine eyes. Luke xix.41,42.

 Jerusalem, prior to the day of Pentecost, had passed through strange and moving scenes, more especially within the previous two-score years. Within and around her had taken place events of vital importance and far-reaching effects, which had caused anxiety to leaders of religion and state. The former were concerned because persistent rumour had divested their long-looked-for Messiah of His glory and triumph, and had wrapped Him in garments of lowliness and humility. The latter were aroused because a kingdom of a new order was about to be established, and its King had already been born. On one side there were predictive whisperings and murmurings regarding the end of Jewish tradition; on the other fears and dark forebodings concerning a usurped throne. One saw the passing away of all ceremonial law, the other the decline and fall of their glorious empire.

 More recently the strange and fearless John the Baptist had come dangerously, near to the city, and his approach had intensified the anxiety, for he openly proclaimed the establishment of a kingdom that would supersede Caesar's. The loud, commanding, penetrating voice of the desert preacher had reached the ears of the rulers, and his message struck terror to their hearts -*"Repent ye, for the kingdom of heaven is at hand. Prepare ye the way of the Lord, make His paths straight."* The leaders of religion discerned in the sound of that voice the death-knell of empty formalism, the end of all typical sacrifice, and the awful spectre of a vacated Temple. Even the select Pharisees and Sadducees had come under the preacher's denunciations—*"O generation of vipers, who hath warned you to flee from the wrath to come? Bring forth therefore fruits meet for repentance: and think not to say within yourselves, We believe Abraham to our father: for I say unto you, that God is able of these stones to raise up children unto Abraham. And now also the axe is laid unto the root of the trees: therefore every tree which bringeth not forth good fruit is hewn down, and cast into the fire."*

The severe tension in religion and state was further accentuated by the news that Jesus the Nazarene, the coming King, was being openly presented to the people, that He had been actually baptised by John in the presence of vast multitudes, and had been publicly declared as the one Mediator between God and man. Time passed on, and nerves, strained to breaking point, were somewhat relaxed through the death of John the Baptist. But it was not long until the inhabitants of the city began to realise that what they had already experienced were but the rumblings preceding the great spiritual and moral earthquakes that were to shake the city to its foundations.

The temporary relaxation through the riddance of John the Baptist is ended, and there are manifold fears within and without, for the ministry of Jesus is confirmed by miracles and signs which John never did. The whole world seemed to be going after Jesus. It would not be long until the common people themselves would acclaim Him King, and as for established religion, it was passing quickly away. Something must be done and that soon, if religion and state are to be saved.

The task of convincing the people in their favour and against Jesus is formidable. How could the people be turned against Him when they saw the result of His touch in delivering and healing? Why, the winds and the waves obey His voice, and even the dead are raised. The only possible way would be to find some discrepancy between His teaching and the teaching of their beloved Moses. A seeming inaccuracy might suffice, because the people loved and revered the Law, and even Moses himself.

Time passes on, and intrigue soon discloses a possible solution. Jesus must die like John the Baptist, and the state combines with religion to erect His cross. Then with fury, malice, and hatred surging around it Christ gives up the ghost amid scenes of ignominy.

The desert preacher is gone, Jesus is dead, the great struggle for existence is now over, and they begin once again to build upon the foundations of false hopes and uncertainties. What irreparable loss could have been saved, what anguish of soul avoided, if only both religion and state had seen in the person of Christ that corn of wheat that was destined to die before bringing forth the inevitable harvest.

Three short days pass—and the lull in the storm proves to be the calm before thunders roll and the lightnings flash. It is the third day, and the news falls like an avalanche upon the city—Jesus is alive, the seal of the Empire broken, the stone is rolled away, and the tomb in which He lay is empty. Difficulties in the city are multiplied, religion and state are unnerved, for they now have to contend with One who had even broken the bonds of death. Far better had they allowed Him to live than to be placed in this nerve-racking dilemma with its unmistakable dark forebodings. Days pass slowly by, and although there are rumours of His being seen and heard by His disciples He does not appear openly as before, and perhaps He never will.

In her bewilderment poor deluded Jerusalem tries to find solace in sleep, and to settle down once more after the past strenuous years. The tranquillity of her dreams is not realised, and under present conditions there is an uncertainty about the future. The day of Pentecost draws near. It is almost fifty days since the day of His resurrection, and the city is filled with the sons of Abraham who have come into it from far and near for the annual celebration of Pentecost. It would not be difficult to say what was the chief subject of conversation. The stranger from afar would enquire diligently of those who lived near concerning the scenes that had taken place in and around the ancient city. A thousand questions were asked and as many answered. Rumours of all kinds were in circulation, and conjectures were clothed in eloquence.

Let us at this juncture try to visualise the scenes at the two central places of worship in the city, just before the dawning of this great day. The one is the magnificent Temple, where everything is in readiness for the great Jewish festival about to be celebrated. On the morrow the priest will stand in flowing robes before the Temple veil, waving, as the custom was, the two wave-loaves which were the firstfruits of harvest. It would be the same veil that had been rent some seven weeks before, exactly at the time when Jesus died. Alas! that which had been rent by the Divine hand, in order to show that the way into His presence was now open, had by this time been sewn together or replaced by the hand of man.

The other place of worship is a plain insignificant upper room where one hundred and twenty disciples of Jesus are gathered. They have been holding a prayer convention in anticipation of an outpouring of the Holy Spirit which their Lord had promised. Tomorrow, the tenth day of their prayer meeting, they will meet as they have done every day since they commenced. There will be no priests officiating, for they need no mediator save Jesus, who is on the Father's throne. There will be no ritual, and very little formality, for each one will simply pour out his or her heart in prayer until the windows of heaven are opened.

We have thus given some idea of the conditions which prevailed in the city of Jerusalem, from the birth of Christ until the day when God ushered in the great dispensation of the Holy Spirit. It is now the day of Pentecost. Nothing unusual happens in the grand Temple, the services are conducted in the same orderly manner as they have been for centuries.

Jerusalem was once more seeking to re, establish the ordinary routine of its normal life, and to settle down undisturbed by the mysterious forces that had troubled her in recent years. These she hoped had been abated, and there would be no recurrence. Then suddenly the heavens were opened right over the upper room, and showers of latter rain descended. The lightning tongues of fire fell, thunderous praise pealed forth, until the ancient city was rocked to and fro by the greatest of spiritual and moral forces. Pictures drawn by the hand of God on Old Testament parchment had suddenly come to life with energising and quickening effect. Biblical type had merged into antitype, and Pentecostal showers were falling, drenching the barren land of religious experience. Rippling rivers of living water that had their source in the far shadows of scriptural prophecy were surging in upon the astonished inhabitants. Fountains of deep, sincere, and sanctified emotion were breaking forth, and thousands were turning to God for salvation through the crucified, risen, and glorified Christ. The moral foundations rocked and false religious structures crashed. Truly the greatest of all spiritual upheavals befell the city.

Chapter 2. The Great Outpouring.

And when the day of Pentecost was fully come, they were all with one accord in one place. And suddenly there came a sound from heaven as of a rushing mighty wind, and it filled all the house where they were sitting. And there appeared unto them cloven tongues like as of fire, and it sat upon each of them. And they were all filled with the Holy Ghost, and began to speak with other tongues, as the Spirit gave them utterance. Acts ii.1-4.

The great day of Pentecost had come and with it the great outpouring. It started, not in the grand Temple, but in the plain upper room. Not with the well-established order of priests, but with the more ordinary and common folk. While the worshippers in the Temple handled the type, the disciples of the upper room were enjoying the antitype. While the former lurked in the shadows of the Old Covenant, the latter partook of the substance of the New. The worshippers in the Temple gazed at pictures of Pentecost while worshippers in the upper room experienced the reality of Pentecost.

Before meditating on the wonders of this exceptional day it would be well for us at this juncture to consider a few of the set feasts of Jehovah in the Old Testament with which the children of Israel were thoroughly acquainted. This will help us to see how blindly they observed ordinances of vital importance without grasping their typical import. Year after year, century after century, the same set feasts of Jehovah had been kept by the children of Israel, but the great doctrinal and practical lessons they were designed to teach seemed to have been lost to the people. Let us glance briefly at three of these set feasts.

Passover.
But at the place which the Lord thy God shall choose to place His Name in, there thou shalt sacrifice the passover at even, at the going down of the sun, at the season that thou earnest forth out of Egypt. Deut.xvi.6.

This was the first of Jehovah's set feasts, for it was the great memorial of redemption and deliverance from the land of Egypt. It was observed in that land by the children of Israel on the fourteenth day of the first month, from which the entire calendar of their sacred year was made anew, for it was their birthday as a new and separate nation. There are many precious details in connection with the Passover feast over which we could muse to our heart's content, but we must pass on to its salient feature. The paschal lamb was the central feature, for it was the spotless victim upon which the stroke of righteous judgment had fallen on that memorable night of deliverance from the land of bondage. The children of Israel, even at the last Passover before Calvary, seemed to have missed its typical import, for they did not see its counterpart in the death of Christ. *Christ our Passover is sacrificed for us; therefore let us keep the feast...1 Cor.v.7,8.*

Firstfruits.
The first of the firstfruits of thy land thou shalt bring into the house of the Lord thy God. Exodus xxiii.19.

This was the third of the set feasts, and it was observed exactly three days from the Feast of Passover. Here again are many interesting details that can provide much thoughtful and helpful meditation, but we can only glance at the sheaf that had been reaped from the fields of ripened harvest which the priest waved before the Lord. This Feast of Firstfruits was no more understood by the people than was the Feast of Passover. Upon the very day on which Christ was raised from the dead the priest in the Temple celebrated the Feast of Firstfruits. Even the rending of the veil which had taken place three days before did not deter him from waving in empty form the sheaf that typified the resurrection of Christ.

But now is Christ risen from the dead, and become the firstfruits of them that slept. 1 Cor.xv.20.

Pentecost Or The Feast Of Weeks.

And thou shalt keep the feast of weeks unto the Lord thy God with a tribute of a freewill offering of thine hand, which thou shalt give unto the Lord thy God, according as the Lord thy God hath blessed thee. Deut.xvi.10.

We now come to the feast that typified the outpouring of the Holy Spirit. This feast is called

Pentecost, which means the fiftieth, because it was held exactly fifty days after the Feast of Firstfruits which we have just considered. It is also called the feast of weeks, because the same period between the two feasts is known as a week of weeks.

Like the others there are many details from which much profitable instruction could be gained, but we shall content ourselves with the main characteristic. Two loaves made of fine flour, fruit of the harvest which had just been gathered in, were waved before the Lord by the priest. The lesson is again lost, and the two loaves, fruit of the new harvest, is not seen in the light of the harvest of souls that was to be brought in as a result of the outpouring of the Spirit on that day. *And when the day of Pentecost was fully come, they were all with one accord in one place. Acts ii.1, Then they that gladly received his word were baptised: and the same day there were added unto them about three thousand souls. Acts ii.41.*

Alas! over nineteen hundred years have rolled on and there are multitudes of professing Christians in our day who make the same mistake and commit the same blunder as the children of Israel did on the day of Pentecost. Year after year the great events of the past are celebrated without grasping their vital significance. Let us briefly mention three.

The Death Of Christ.
On Good Friday hearts the world over are moved with compassion towards the Man of Calvary, and eyes everywhere are turned in the direction of that central Figure. But how few seem to know the secret of identification with Him.

I am crucified with Christ: nevertheless I live; yet not I, but Christ liveth in me : and the life which I now live in the flesh I live by the faith of the Son of God, who loved me, and gave Himself for me. Gal.ii.20.

The Resurrection Of Christ.
Eastertide is resurrection time, when special sermons are preached, and the whole earth resounds with the song of resurrection in commemoration of that great day. Yet relatively how small is the number that can claim to be definitely justified.

Therefore being justified by faith, we have peace with God through our Lord Jesus Christ: By whom also we have access by faith into this grace wherein we stand, and rejoice in hope of the glory of God. Rom.v.1,2.

The Outpouring Of The Spirit.

Whitsuntide, the Pentecostal period, is celebrated year after year by vast multitudes, yet it is amazing to find how many deliberately reject an outpouring of the Spirit akin to that which the disciples at Pentecost experienced.

Ye stiffnecked and uncircumcised in heart and ears, ye do always resist the Holy Ghost: as your fathers did, so do ye. Acts vii.51.

The worshippers at the Temple celebrated the various feasts which foreshadowed the great events connected with the plan of redemption, but they missed the experiences and benefits of that plan. Many professing Christians of to-day, while celebrating those great events of the past, are also missing the experiences and benefits of the great plan of redemption.

The Supernatural In The Old Testament.

The momentous events of the day of Pentecost, associated as they were with the crucifixion and resurrection of Christ, were unparalleled in history. There had been times when Israel had witnessed supernatural manifestations of Jehovah, but nothing like what the inhabitants of Jerusalem saw and heard on that day. Inspired history had acquainted the people with outstanding supernatural events, such as Israel's miraculous deliverance from Egypt, the dividing of the Red Sea, the miracles of the nation in the wilderness, the marvels of Sinai, the walls of Jericho falling, the effect of the prophet's mantle on the waters of Jordan, of fire descending in answer to prayer, and many other remarkable things; but they had never read of such a phenomenal visitation as they now witnessed. It was something so mighty, so out of the ordinary, that the people were overwhelmed with amazement.

The Supernatural In The Upper Room.
It started in the upper room, probably the same room in which Jesus and the disciples had kept the Passover feast some seven weeks before. It came as a rushing mighty wind upon the disciples; it filled the whole place where they were sitting, and then, breaking loose like a cyclone, it passed over the city with such velocity that thousands were carried into the spiritual kingdom of God. We shall now consider the effect that the Spirit had upon the waiting disciples in the upper room.

The Effect Upon The Human Faculties.
And suddenly there came a sound from heaven as of a rushing mighty wind, and it filled all the house where they were sitting. And there appeared unto them cloven tongues like as of fire, and it sat upon each of them. And they were all filled with the Holy Ghost, and began to speak with other tongues. Acts ii.2-4.

The effect upon the ear.
And suddenly there came a sound.
The disciples had been tuning in to Heaven during those ten days of waiting, and their ears had become sensitive enough to catch the sound when Heaven began broadcasting the Pentecostal blessing.

The effect upon the eye.
And there appeared unto them...
They saw the cloven tongues like as of fire that had come to sit on each of them. There was something more here than the look of faith. They had read of manifestations of

the dazzling brightness of God in Tabernacle and Temple; now they saw a glimpse of that glory right in their very midst.

The effect upon the mortal body.

And they were all filled with the Holy Ghost.

This was the fulfilment of their Lord's promise—"*He that believeth on Me, as the scripture hath said, out of him shall flow rivers of living water.*" It was no mere filling by faith, the filling they received affected spirit, soul and body.

The effect upon the vocal organs.

And they began to speak with other tongues.

This was a manifestation never before experienced by anyone, not even in the days of their Lord. It was a distinct sign and gift peculiar to the dispensation that was being ushered in that very day.

The Effect Upon The World.

The disciples in the upper room were that day clothed with power to reap in a spiritual harvest, the antitype of that which the sons of Israel had come to celebrate. Three thousand souls were saved, upon another day five thousand, and so on, while the reapers in the golden harvest field magnified the Lord. They not only received power to reap, they were endued with power that enabled them to contend for the faith, and to go forward in the strength of the Lord. Had not Christ said, "*Upon this rock I will build My Church, and the gates of hell shall not prevail against it?*" These words, so much misunderstood by people to-day, were rightly understood by them, for they went forth, and gates, however formidable, had to give way before them. The gates of sin, sickness, unbelief, misrepresentation, and opposition went down before the onward march of the triumphant Early Church. As a result of the anointed Word cities and towns were turned upside down, prison foundations shook and their doors flew open, while kings and emperors feared before the dynamic of the Early Church message. We shall now endeavour to give a main outline of the teaching concerning this Pentecostal Outpouring.

The Promise Before Calvary.
If ye love Me, keep My commandments,
And I will pray the Father, and He shall give you another Comforter, that He may abide with you for ever; even the Spirit of truth; whom the world cannot receive, because it seeth Him not, neither knoweth Him: but ye know Him; for He dwelleth with you, and shall be in you. John xiv.15-17.
Our Lord had just mentioned the fact of His going away, and the disciples were troubled in heart. They had spent something like three and a half years in His company, and He had been their best friend. They had brought their difficulties and problems to Him, and He had solved them. They had sat at His feet as disciples, and He had fed them with the bread of life. They had come to Him in drought, and He had quenched their thirst with living water. He was everything to them, and when He talks of going away their hearts are almost broken. Then in the midst of their sorrow He gives them the promise of another Comforter.

The Promise After Calvary.
And, behold, I send the promise of My Father upon you: but tarry ye in the city of Jerusalem, until ye be endued with power from on high. Luke xxiv.49.
Calvary is now an accomplished fact; the tomb is empty, and He stands in their midst as risen Lord. We have often

thought of this first soul-stirring Bible reading after the Resurrection. He had opened their understanding many times before during the days that preceded Calvary, and their hearts had been strangely moved. But on this occasion no earthly language could possibly express the burning within that must have been. There He stands, with the same old Book from which to teach, but under vastly different circumstances. It was as risen Lord that He confirmed the promise of a Pentecostal Outpouring.

The Promise Of The Father.

And it shall come to pass afterward, that I will pour out My Spirit upon all flesh; and your sons and your daughters shall prophesy, your old men shall dream dreams, your young men shall see visions: And also upon the servants and upon the handmaids in those days will I pour out My Spirit.—Joel ii.28,29.

We can almost hear Him read or quote this prophecy in the Book of Joel, for it was undoubtedly this promise that He speaks of. They were to tarry in Jerusalem until it would be fulfilled—the very place of His crucifixion, the very scenes of His suffering, and in the midst of those who had crucified Him? Yes! As soon as they should receive the blessing they were to begin to tell forth the glorious message of love and salvation even to those who crucified Him. The very carpenters who made the cross were to be told that He had prepared a throne for them. The person who plaited the crown of thorns was to be told that a crown of glory was waiting to be placed upon his brow. The soldier who opened His side with the spear was to know that there was a much nearer way to His heart. All were to be told that He had voluntarily laid down His life for their sins, and that He had taken it again for their justification.

Steps Leading To The Fulfilment.

In the first chapter of the Acts of the Apostles we believe the Holy Spirit has with the utmost precision indicated the steps leading up to the Pentecostal blessing of chapter ii. Let us look at them briefly.

Fellowship with a risen Lord.

To whom also He shewed Himself alive after His passion by many infallible proofs, being seen of them forty days, and speaking of the things pertaining to the kingdom of God. Acts i.3.

The disciples had fellowship with the risen Lord because they were believing disciples. They were born again and had received Him as Saviour, hence the reason why they could commune with Him after the resurrection.

The first and second steps: Identification with Him in death must precede fellowship with Him in life.

I am crucified with Christ: nevertheless I live; yet not I, but Christ liveth in me: and the life which I now live in the flesh I live by the faith of the Son of God, who loved me, and gave Himself for me. Gal.ii.20.

Therefore the first step towards the outpouring of the Spirit is salvation; the second is communion with the risen Christ.

The third step: Obedience.

Then returned they unto Jerusalem from the mount called Olivet, which is from Jerusalem a sabbath day's journey. Acts i.12.

They made their way toward the centre in which the promise was to be fulfilled, and the disciples by their obedience manifested their faith in His Word.

The Company Who Tarried.

And when they were come in, they went up into an upper

room, where abode both Peter, and James, and John, and Andrew, Philip, and Thomas, Bartholomew, and Matthew, James the son of Alphæus, and Simon Zelotes, and Judas the brother of James. Acts i.13.

Men and women of different temperaments and with different characteristics—among them Peter the impulsive, John the beloved, James the stoic, and Mary the mother of our Lord. All waiting for the coming of the great and glorious day.

The Attitude Of The Company.
These all continued with one accord in prayer and supplication, with the women, and Mary the mother of Jesus, and with His brethren, Acts i.14.

The tenth day of the prayer convention came when the heavens were opened, and each one received a definite baptism of the Holy Spirit in fulfilment of the promise.

The Promise Fulfilled.
And when the day of Pentecost was fully come... they were all filled with the Holy Ghost... Acts ii.1,4.

The Effect Upon The People.
Now when this was noised abroad, the multitude came together, and were confounded, because that every man heard them speak in his own language... And they were all amazed, and were in doubt, saying one to another, What meaneth this? Others mocking said, These men are full of new wine. Acts ii.6,12,13.

Peter Testifies To The Fulfilment Of Prophecy.
But Peter, standing up with the eleven, lifted up his voice, and said unto them, Ye men of Judaea, and all ye that dwell at Jerusalem, be this known unto you, and hearken to my words: For these are not drunken, as ye suppose, seeing it is

but the third hour of the day. But this is that which was spoken by the prophet Joel. Acts ii.14-16.

Two Commands And A Promise To Every Sinner.
Then Peter said unto them, Repent, and be baptised every one of you in the Name of Jesus Christ for the remission of sins, and ye shall receive the gift of the Holy Ghost. Acts ii.38.

The Scope Of The Promise.
For the promise is unto you, and to your children, and to all that are afar off, even as many as the Lord our God shall call. Acts ii.39.

Thus we have given a brief outline of the teaching concerning the baptism of the Holy Spirit which is the birthright of every believer. All who take the steps in the first chapter of the Acts of the Apostles can expect to receive the Pentecostal blessing of the second.

Chapter 3. The Holy Spirit Personality—Terms—Views.

Study to shew thyself approved unto God, a workman that needeth not to be ashamed, rightly dividing the Word of truth. 2Tim.ii.15.

Ignorance concerning the Personality and work of the Holy Spirit has resulted in wrong, foolish and unintelligible conceptions. He has been regarded as the source of all kinds of inspiration, as the mysterious influence that inspires poets, musicians and artists, saints and sinners alike, and as a breath that pervades the atmosphere of a religious service. We well remember the illustration used by one who claimed to be a minister of the Gospel when dealing with the
subject: "You have watched the musician draw his bow over the strings of the violin, and have been entranced at the exquisite melody produced. You have been enamoured of the paintings that speak with inaudible voice to the human soul, and have taken flight on the wings of poetry to realms of untold bliss. That invisible influence behind the bow, and the brush, and in the poet, is none other than the Holy Ghost."
It did not occur to the preacher that soul-stirring music, entrancing paintings, and fanciful poetry are sometimes produced by sinners of the deepest dye. The work of the Spirit upon such characters is that which produces conviction of sin. This is the only relationship we see between the Holy Spirit and sinners, until they repent and turn to God.
Illustrations such as these but reveal great ignorance,

and are calculated to obscure the Personality of the Holy Spirit, and to make sinners believe that His work is not to convict of sin, but to console in sin.

The Holy Spirit Is A Person.

This is proved by the application to Him in Scripture of personal pronouns:

But when the Comforter is come, whom I will send unto you from the Father, even the Spirit of truth, which proceedeth from the Father, He shall testify of Me. John xv.26.

Nevertheless I tell you the truth; It is expedient for you that I go away: for if I go not away, the Comforter will not come unto you; but if I depart, I will send Him unto you. And when He is come He will reprove the world of sin, and of righteousness, and of judgment, John xvi.7,8.

He has personal faculties.

He can speak, see, and hear.

As they ministered to the Lord, and fasted, the Holy Ghost said, Separate Me Barnabas and Saul for the work whereunto I have called them. Acts xiii.2.

So they, being sent forth by the Holy Ghost, departed unto Seleucia; and from thence they sailed to Cyprus. Acts xiii.4.

He has emotions.

He can be grieved.

And grieve not the Holy Spirit of God, whereby ye are sealed unto the day of redemption. Eph.iv.30.

He has a will.

He distributes miraculous gifts according to His will.

But all these worketh that one and the selfsame Spirit, dividing to every man severally as He will. 1Cor.xii.11. The Deity of the Holy Spirit is clearly demonstrated by His associations with the Father and with the Son.

He is eternal.

Without beginning and without ending.

How much more shall the blood of Christ, who through the eternal Spirit offered Himself without spot to God, purge your conscience from dead works to serve the living God. Heb.ix.14.

He is omnipotent.

Author of the body of Jesus of Nazareth.

And the angel answered and said unto her, The Holy Ghost shall come upon thee, and the power of the Highest shall overshadow thee: therefore also that holy thing which shall be born of thee shall be called the Son of God. Luke i.35.

He is omniscient.

Guides into all truth.

I have yet many things to say unto you, but ye cannot bear them now. Howbeit when He, the Spirit of truth, is come, He will guide you into all truth: for He shall not speak of Himself; but whatsoever He shall hear, that shall He speak: and He will shew you things to come. John xvi.12,13.

He is omnipresent.

Dwells with and within believers everywhere.

And I will pray the Father, and He shall give you another Comforter, that He may abide with you for ever; even the Spirit of truth; whom the world cannot receive, because it seeth Him not, neither knoweth Him: but ye know Him; for He dwelleth with you, and shall be in you. John xiv.16,17.

Both Old and New Testaments abound with evidence that proves the Deity and Personality of the Holy Ghost.

The Great Need Of To-Day.

The great need of believers in particular and the Church in general is an outpouring of the Holy Ghost with power to cope with the inrush of unbelief, worldliness, and indifference that has invaded the professing Church through the avenues of modernistic teaching. The present age is one of materialism, and it can only be effectively dealt with by the demonstration of the power of the essentially supernatural and dynamic forces of the Christian religion. We are convinced that the way to power in the Church is along the lines of the individual baptism of the Holy Ghost. In order to get a right perspective of scriptural teaching it would be well for us to consider the views of the various schools of thought on the subject.

Varied Views Concerning Terms.

Some teachers maintain that each of the following terms used in connection with the operations of the Holy Ghost presents a new aspect of truth and that they are not interchangeable.

(a) Baptism, (b) Indwelling, (c) Gift, (d) Earnest, (e) Filling, (f) Anointing, (g) Sealing, (h) Outpouring.

The four that are definitely mentioned in the first and second chapters of the Acts of the Apostles will suffice for our consideration at this juncture.

They are as follow:

Baptism.

For John truly baptised with water; but ye shall be baptised with the Holy Ghost not many days hence. Acts i.5.

Filling.

And they were all filled with the Holy Ghost, and began to speak with other tongues, as the Spirit gave them utterance. Acts ii.4.

Outpouring.

And it shall come to pass in the last days, saith God, I will pour out of My Spirit upon all flesh: and your sons and your daughters shall prophesy, and your young men shall see visions, and your old men shall dream dreams: And on My servants and on My handmaidens I will pour out in those days of My Spirit; and they shall prophesy. Acts ii.17,18.

Gift.

Then Peter said unto them, Repent, and be baptised every one of you in the Name of Jesus Christ for the remission of sins, and ye shall receive the gift of the Holy Ghost. Acts ii.38.

There is a simple and decisive way of proving whether these terms are interchangeable or not. The correct answer to the following question will settle the matter once and for all. Do the terms *baptism, filling, outpouring,* and *gift* refer to one and the same experience? If the answer is in the negative, then they are not interchangeable; if the answer is in the affirmative, then the terms are interchangeable.

The baptism of the Spirit.

Let us now put this test to the first term. The *baptism* that was mentioned by our Lord in Acts i.5 was most assuredly that which the disciples experienced on the one great day of Pentecost,

when He said, "*Ye shall be baptised with the Holy Ghost not many days hence.*" He must have been referring to that Pentecostal experience which actually occurred ten days afterwards. Therefore that Pentecostal experience was termed a *baptism*.

The filling of the Spirit.

The experience that was termed a *baptism* by our Lord is now called a *filling* by the inspired writer of the Acts of the Apostles. Therefore that same Pentecostal experience was termed a *baptism* and also a *filling*.

The outpouring of the Spirit.

Peter on the day of Pentecost actually explained that the disciples were experiencing an *outpouring* of the Spirit in fulfilment of an Old Testament prophecy. Therefore the same Pentecostal experience was termed a *baptism*, a *filling*, and an *outpouring.*

The gift of the Spirit.

The Scripture clearly teaches that up to and during the days of our Lord the Holy Spirit had not been given. It also affirms that the Holy Spirit was definitely shed forth on the day of Pentecost. In the light of these negative and positive affirmations it is only reasonable to conclude that what the disciples experienced on the Day of Pentecost was the *gift* of the Holy Spirit. Peter in his message to all who would henceforth repent and be baptised confirmed this view when he
said, "*And ye shall receive the gift of the Holy Ghost.*" He made the promise because the Holy Spirit had been given that day. This is further confirmed by Peter's statement in Acts xi.16,17, where the figures, *baptism* and *gift*, are shown to be identical, for they were both used to describe the one experience at Pentecost. Therefore that same Pentecostal experience was termed a *baptism, a filling, an outpouring,* and a *gift.*

Different Views Concerning The Time Of Reception Of The Spirit.

There are two main schools of thought. One maintains that the gift of the Holy Spirit is identical with the gift of eternal life, and that a person cannot be in a regenerated state without the gift of the Holy Spirit. The other affirms that the gift of the Holy Spirit is quite distinct from the gift of eternal life, and that a person can be in a regenerated state without possessing the gift of the

Holy Spirit. Here again we have a simple yet decisive way of settling the question. If there is any record in the Acts of the Apostles to show that persons were saved who subsequently received the gift of the Holy Spirit, then the view of the second school is maintained. We believe that the Samaritan revival in the eighth chapter of the Acts proves the case for the second school of thought without a doubt, as the following facts will demonstrate.

Philip the Evangelist at Samaria.
Then Philip went down to the city of Samaria, and preached Christ unto them. Acts viii.5.
The attitude of the people.
And the people with one accord gave heed unto those things which Philip spake, hearing and seeing the miracles which he did. Acts viii.6.
Miracles and signs were in evidence.
For unclean spirits, crying with loud voice, came out of many that were possessed with them: and many taken with palsies, and that were lame, were healed. Acts viii.7.
Joyousness was one of the characteristics.
And there was great joy in that city. Acts viii.8.
The converts passed through the waters of baptism.
But when they believed Philip preaching the things concerning the kingdom of God, and the Name of Jesus Christ, they were baptised, both men and women. Acts viii.12.
Up to this point the Holy Ghost had not fallen, for Peter and John were with the Apostles at Jerusalem.
Now when the apostles which were at Jerusalem heard that Samaria had received the word of God, they sent unto them Peter and John. Acts viii.14.
Peter and John arrive at Samaria.
Who, when they were come down, prayed for them, that they

might receive the Holy Ghost: (For as yet He was fallen upon none of them: only they were baptised in the Name of the Lord Jesus). Then laid they their hands on them, and they received the Holy Ghost. Acts viii.15-17.

There are other cases in Scripture which will come up for careful consideration in due course.

Different Views Regarding The Purpose For Which The Holy Spirit Is Given.

There are two main schools of thought concerning the purpose for which the Holy Spirit is given to individual believers. One holds that the definite reception of the Spirit after conversion is identical with an experience called sanctification, or the experience of a clean heart. They believe that at conversion eternal life is received as a gift, and the person is delivered from his sins. But at the reception of the Spirit the same person is delivered from what is called inbred sin. The other school of thought claims that at conversion the person is made a new creature in Christ, that he is cleansed from all sin by the blood of Christ, and that he receives the subsequent gift of the Holy Spirit to empower him for service. We belong to the second school, for our contention is that the Holy Spirit does not deliver or cleanse from sin of any kind. The Holy Spirit convicts of sin, but it is the Blood that cleanses.

But if we walk in the light, as He is in the light, we have fellowship one with another, and the blood of Jesus Christ His Son cleanseth us from all sin. 1 John i.7.

Those who teach, that until believers receive the gift of the Holy Spirit they are in an unsanctified state, must, in order to be consistent, teach that the mother of our Lord was in an unsanctified state when Jesus was born, for she was one of the one hundred and twenty who received the gift of the Holy Ghost on the day of Pentecost.

Diverse Views As To The Effect Of The Spirit On The Mortal Body.

In this connection there are three main schools of thought. The first teaches that every person who receives the gift of the Holy Spirit will have the sign of speaking in tongues; the second, that everyone who receives should have some definite supernatural manifestation of the Spirit in the mortal body, not necessarily the sign of the speaking in tongues; while the third stands for the reception of the Spirit by faith without any outward physical sign. The second view is the scriptural one; it safeguards against the possibility of a seeker after the gift of the Spirit missing the blessing, and also against the extravagances that might be entailed by a mere reaching out for an initial sign of speaking in tongues, which the Scriptures do not warrant. Tongues, or glossolalia, in Acts ii.1-4, as well as in every other instance in the Acts of the Apostles, is a gift as well as a sign, proved conclusively by the fact that it is not in the aorist but in the imperfect tense, which shows that it is to be repeated.

The reason why persons who receive this gift at the baptism of the Spirit do not afterwards speak in tongues is occasioned by the lack of its exercise. It is impromptu at the baptism, but afterwards almost entirely under the control of the speaker.

The following scripture confirms this view— 1Corinthians xii.30, *"Have all the gifts of healing? do all speak with tongues? do all interpret?"*

Speaking in tongues was as frequently given as a sign at the baptism of the Spirit in the days of the Apostles as it is to-day, but the silence of Scripture on the question of it being the initial sign negatives the claim that it must necessarily follow in every case. When we come to the Samaritan revival the Scripture positively declares that the converts received the Holy Spirit by the laying on of the Apostles' hands, yet there is no mention of the sign of speaking in tongues.

Insistence upon this particular sign for every seeker, in face of these positive and negative affirmations of Scripture on the subject, means the violation of the reasonable and logical law that should govern the right dividing of the Word of truth. The claim based upon precept and example that tongues is the initial sign of the Baptism is not valid, because it is not stated to be the example in Acts iv, nor in Acts viii. Even if tongues were mentioned in both these scriptures it would not be a sound method to build doctrines on example. But if the speaking in tongues is not mentioned in the account of the Samaritan revival, there was undoubtedly some kind of physical manifestation as a result of the reception of the Holy Spirit, for Simon saw the effect of

the laying on of the Apostles' hands. It would be most difficult to harmonise the view, that the gift of the Holy Spirit can be received by faith apart from any physical effect, with the declaration of our Lord in the seventh chapter of John:

If any man thirst, let him come unto Me, and drink. He that believeth on Me, as the Scripture hath said, out of him shall flow rivers of living water. (But this spake He of the Spirit, which they that believe on Him should receive: for the Holy Ghost was not yet given; because that Jesus was not yet glorified).

Chapter 4. The Spirit Of Christ And The Holy Spirit.

Now if any man have not the Spirit of Christ he is none of His. Rom.viii.9. Have ye received the Holy Ghost since ye believed? Acts xix.2.

Seldom are our minds directed to the difference between the Spirit of Christ and the Holy Spirit, yet it is impossible to have an intelligent understanding of the New Testament Scriptures without recognising such a difference. The way to a right conclusion of the matter is by comparing scripture with scripture, and thus allowing the inspired commentary to explain itself. Before doing so, it would be well for us to look briefly at the views of some who are not disposed to agree with such a difference. Some Christian teachers maintain that the scripture in Romans viii. 9, *"Now if any man have not the Spirit of Christ, he is none of His,"* emphatically declares that it is impossible to be a believer without having the Holy Spirit. The gift of the Holy Spirit, they say, is identical with regeneration. We maintain that there is a difference, and that the scripture in Romans viii. 9 refers to the Spirit of Christ, and not to the Holy Spirit. We teach that the former takes up His abode in the believer at regeneration, and that the latter can only be received by those already regenerated. The correct answers to the following questions should decide the matter without difficulty.

Firstly, does the Scripture state the fixed time

when the outpouring of the Holy Ghost first took place? The answer is given by the inspired writer of the Acts of the Apostles, and by the preacher of Pentecost: *And when the day of Pentecost was fully come, they were all with one accord in one place... And they were all filled with the Holy Ghost, and began to speak with other tongues as the Spirit gave them utterance. Acts ii.1,4. Peter, standing up with the eleven, lifted up his voice, and said unto them, Ye men of Judaea, and all ye that dwell at Jerusalem, be this known unto you, and hearken to my words : for these are not drunken, as ye suppose, seeing it is but the third hour of the day. But this is that which was spoken by the prophet Joel; And it shall come to pass in the last days, saith God, I will pour out of My Spirit upon all flesh... Acts ii.14-17.*

Ye men of Israel, hear these words; Jesus of Nazareth, a man approved of God among you by miracles and wonders and signs... Ye have taken, and by wicked hands have crucified and slain... This Jesus hath God raised up, whereof we all are witnesses. Therefore being by the right hand of God exalted, and having received of the Father the promise of the Holy Ghost, He hath shed forth this, which ye now see and hear. Acts ii.22,23,32,33.

By negative assertion as well as positive the Scriptures emphasise the time when the Holy Spirit was given. Our Lord clearly stated in the Gospels that the Holy Spirit had not been given even during His earthly ministry; it was an event reserved for future days.

In the last day, that great day of the feast, Jesus stood and cried, saying, If any man thirst, let him come unto Me and drink. He that believeth on Me, as the Scripture hath said, out of him shall flow rivers of living water. (But this spake He of the Spirit, which they that believe on Him should receive: for the Holy Ghost was not yet given; because that Jesus was not yet glorified.) John vii.37-39.

Thus the answer to the first question is in the affirmative. The Holy Spirit had certainly come upon exceptional individuals for specific purposes before the day of Pentecost, but He was not given in the general sense until that day.

Secondly, were there regenerated persons on earth before the Holy Spirit was given on the day of Pentecost? The answer to this question is also in the affirmative, for the evidences of regeneration are seen in the disciples before the day of Pentecost.

Spiritual relationship established.

Regeneration, which establishes the spiritual family relationship between seekers and God, was experienced by the mere acceptance of Christ as Saviour long before the dispensation of the Holy Ghost.

He came unto His own, and His own received Him not. But as many as received Him, to them gave He power to become the sons of God, even to them that believe on His Name. Which were born, not of blood, nor of the. will of the flesh, nor of the will of man, but of God. John i.11-13.

All who received Him were born of God, and it does not say that they had to wait for regeneration until the Holy Ghost would be given on the day of Pentecost. At the beginning of His public ministry, our Lord met Nicodemus, a ruler of the Jews. During his conversation with him He points to the one door through which all that enter His spiritual kingdom must pass, namely, *the new birth.*

The door was there, ready to be opened by faith. Not a word is mentioned about waiting some three years until the Holy Spirit should be given. Let us now look for evidences of true regeneration in the lives of the disciples

who lived on the earth before the Holy Spirit was given:
They were not of the world.
I have given them Thy Word; and the world hath hated them, because they are not of the world, even as I am not of the world.—John xvii.14.
Their standing in the world had altered; some remarkable change in each person of the company prayed for had been brought about by the regeneration of their souls. They had been born of the last Adam; they were in the world, but not of it; affections that were once set on things below had been transferred to things above.
They were spiritually clean.
Now ye are clean through the Word which I have spoken unto you.—John xv.3.
They had not always been considered thus; like others, in their unsaved state they were likened unto an unclean thing, whose righteousness was as filthy rags. These garments had been discarded for the righteousness which is of faith, the garment woven in the mind of God before the foundation of the world, on the looms of Bethlehem and Calvary.
As part of the true Vine they were to bear fruit.
Abide in Me, and I in you. As the branch cannot bear fruit of itself, except it abide in the vine; no more can ye, except ye abide in Me. I am the Vine, ye are the branches: he that abideth in Me, and I in him, the same bringeth forth much fruit: for without Me ye can do nothing. John xv.4,5.
Herein is My Father glorified, that ye bear much fruit; so shall ye be My disciples. John xv.8.
Unless they were branches of the true Vine, bearing fruit would be an impossibility. One would as well expect to see a lily growing out of a thistle seed, as to find the fruit of the Spirit in the lives of the unregenerate.

But these disciples were in Christ; they had their life, and drew their sustenance from Him, and it was quite natural for them to produce the fruit of the Spirit—love, joy, peace, long-suffering, gentleness, goodness, faith, meekness, temperance; for they were of
the Lord's planting.

They were commissioned to evangelise.
As Thou hast sent Me into the world, even so have I also sent them into the world. John xvii:18.
Who could imagine for a moment that those ordained by our Lord as ministers of the Word to others were unsaved? Those entrusted with the Gospel message should certainly give proof of its transforming power in their own lives. These disciples were to ring out a message of life to a
dying world; they were to carry words of creative power, by which they had themselves been born again.

They were taught how to pray.
And He said unto them, When ye pray, say, Our Father, which art m heaven. Luke xi.2.
The ground of prayer was their relationship to God. If they had not been born into His family, the Master would not be found instructing them in prayer. With Him they shared what is the privilege of every true believer. It was not merely a matter of framing sentences, and going through some prescribed form. They were in touch with the Divine; in His presence they poured out the unutterable gushings of their full hearts, and breathed in the life that would sustain them.

Christ was glorified in them.
And all Mine are Thine, and Thine are Mine, and I am glorified in them. John xvii.10.
Surely Christ could not be glorified in un-regenerate

followers; only consecrated beings could have become vessels containing heavenly treasure. They were by this time yielded servants of obedience unto righteousness, and their bodies were temples for God to dwell in.

They had fellowship with the risen Christ.
To whom also He shewed Himself alive after His passion by many infallible proofs, being seen of them forty days, and speaking of the things pertaining to the kingdom of God. Acts i.3.
Our Lord only revealed Himself to believers after the Resurrection. The last glimpse unbelievers had of Him was upon the cross. No unregenerate soul saw Him after the heart-rending scenes of the Crucifixion. The privilege of fellowship and communion with Him is ever confined to those who are prepared to be identified with Him in His death.

They were promised another Comforter.
And I will pray the Father, and He shall send you another Comforter, that He may abide with you for ever; even the Spirit of Truth; whom the world cannot receive. John xiv.16,17.
By "*the world*" is meant the unregenerate. Unless they were translated from the kingdom of darkness into the kingdom of God's dear Son, they were in no fit condition to receive the Holy Spirit. He will only come to abide in sanctified vessels. These disciples had experienced their spiritual translation and had already yielded themselves to the service of their Lord, because they were not of the world. Therefore they were commanded to tarry until the Comforter should come.

    Long before the great outpouring of the Holy Spirit at Pentecost, there were those who had experienced the new birth. We look back into Old Testament times and find prophets who were indwelt by the Spirit of Christ, and so of course must have been regenerated. Peter testifies to this fact (1Pet.i.11): "*The Spirit of Christ which was in them [the prophets] did signify when He testified beforehand the sufferings of Christ, and the glory that should follow.*" Long before His blood was shed

upon Calvary there were individuals who had accepted God's way of salvation, and were born from above.

The first creation being marred had to be remade before man could have fellowship and oneness with God.

At the entrance of the garden from which the first Adam was expelled, we see the Cherubim and the flaming sword, guarding the way to the tree of life. Between God and the fallen creation was the weapon to pierce and slay. If reconciliation and oneness was to be brought about, it had to come by the Lord passing through the sword and fire to reach the fallen ones. Here we see a picture of Calvary's Cross drawn by the unerring hand of the Holy Spirit. The outcasts were brought face to face with the fact that life could only come to them as a result of death.

Someone had to be pierced and bruised in order to forge the link that could unite them to God. Here veiled in type was Christ, the promised Redeemer. Through death there was the possibility not only of being reinstated in an earthly paradise, but of possessing Divine life, something that they had never experienced before. Here was the door leading into the realms of the new creation. They could, by accepting God's way, become the children of God, having the Spirit of His Son shed abroad in their hearts.

In the lamb offered as a sacrifice by Abel, their son, we see prefigured the One who, of His own will, left the brightness of His Father's glory and passed, when the fullness of time was come, through death on Calvary, in order that all who would believe might be saved. Abel, we are told in the eleventh chapter of Hebrews, obtained witness that he was righteous. He had to come to God through the righteousness of Christ, which the sacrificial lamb foreshadowed. Being righteous, he must have been born again—only a regenerated person could be termed righteous— and if born again, he must have become a son of God, and if a son, he must have possessed the Spirit of God's Son. *"Now if any man have not the Spirit of Christ he is none of His."* (Rom. viii. 9).

Persons who believed God, before the work of redemption was actually accomplished at Calvary, were regenerated through the Redeemer, to whom the types pointed forward. Those who believe God on this side of the Cross are regenerated through the crucified Christ, of whom the breaking of bread and drinking of wine is a reminder (1Cor.xi.23-26). Christ, and He alone, is the Door that leads into the spiritual realm.

Are we to suppose for a moment that the disciples, who were our Lord's bosom friends and companions, were un-regenerated persons? Are we to conclude that the first breaking-of-bread service was celebrated by un-regenerated disciples? Speaking reverently, are we to believe that the holy virgin, who was privileged to bring into the world the offspring of God and the Saviour of mankind, was unregenerate? No! No! Let men take time to think before they are entangled in the meshes of flimsy and illogical conclusions.

In the scriptures considered we have abundant evidence of the new birth before the Holy Ghost came to take up His abode in temples not made with hands. What Christians receive at regeneration is the Spirit of Christ.

God sent forth His Son, made of a woman, made under the law, to redeem them that were under the law, that we might receive the adoption of sons. And because ye are sons, God hath sent forth the Spirit of His Son into your hearts, crying, Abba, Father. Gal.iv.4-6.

The son of the first Adam comes burdened to the Cross. He pleads for pardon through One who in the fullness of time came to bear away his sin. He is forgiven and is immediately conscious of his new relationship. He is suddenly awakened to the fact that he is, there and then, made a son of God. The Spirit of Christ is shed abroad in his heart, and cries, "*Abba, Father.*" There are also instances in the Acts of the Apostles where the Holy Spirit was received subsequent to regeneration after the day of Pentecost. These I have dealt with in other chapters of this book. If the disciples in Acts viii. had not received the Spirit of Christ until hands were laid upon them in verse 17 they must have been previously baptised in the Name of the Lord Jesus when they were "*none of His.*" If the disciples in Acts xix. had not received the Spirit of Christ until Paul laid his hands upon them in verse 6, they too must have been baptised in the

Name of the Lord Jesus when they were "*none of His.*"

In conclusion let me draw your attention to the change in metaphor used by our Lord when speaking of regeneration first, and later on, of the baptism of the Holy Ghost.

You all know the story of the woman at the well of Samaria (John iv.4-42). The words: "*He must needs go through Samaria,"* reveal the deep longing in the Lord's compassionate heart to satisfy the soul thirst of even one sinner. Under the burning Eastern sun, He wended His way to the city, passing en route the ancient well of Jacob. Being wearied with His journey, He sat on the well, and a poor sin-burdened woman came along at a most unusual hour, carrying her water-pot. His request for a drink is met with *"How is it that Thou, being a Jew, askest drink of me, which am a woman of Samaria? for the Jews have no dealings with the Samaritans."* Using water as a symbol of everlasting life, Jesus immediately showed her the blessedness of having the thirst of the soul quenched.

Note carefully His reply, *"If thou knewest the gift of God, and who it is that saith to thee, Give Me to drink, thou wouldest have asked of Him, and He would have given thee living water."* Every careful reader of the Word will admit that the Lord was speaking of eternal life which could only be obtained as a gift. It was likened unto a well springing up, whose gushing waters kept the soul in perpetual satisfaction.

Later on in John vii.37,38, we find our Lord's last public utterance: *"In the last day, that great day of the feast, Jesus stood and cried, saying: If any man thirst, let him come unto Me, and drink. He that believeth on Me, as the Scripture hath said, out of him shall flow rivers of living water."* He is speaking here of the gift of the Holy Ghost which believers alone could receive. He likens this gift unto rivers of living water flowing from the innermost part of the being. It is clearly stated that this blessing could only be received at a future time, thus proving conclusively that there is a difference between receiving the Spirit of Christ, and receiving the Holy

Ghost. It was a *well of living water* in John iv; here, in John vii, *rivers of living water*.

The gift of eternal life when the Spirit of Christ comes in to abide was experienced by the disciples before the day of Pentecost. The gift of the Holy Spirit was experienced by these same disciples on the day of Pentecost.

God's great gift to the unregenerate is the Spirit of Christ. God's great gift to the regenerate is the Holy Spirit.

Chapter 5. More Than Twenty Years After Pentecost.

Believers who had not Received the Holy Ghost

And it came to pass, that, while Apollos was at Corinth, Paul having passed through the upper coasts came to Ephesus: and finding certain disciples, he said unto them, Have ye received the Holy Ghost since ye believed? And they said unto him, We have not so much as heard whether there be any Holy Ghost. And he said unto them: Unto what then were ye baptised? And they said, Unto John's baptism. Then said Paul, John verily baptised with the baptism of repentance, saying unto the people, that they should believe on Him which should come after him, that is, on Christ Jesus. When they heard this, they were baptised in the Name of the Lord Jesus. And when Paul had laid his hands upon them, the Holy Ghost came on them; and they spake with tongues, and prophesied. And all the men were about twelve.
—Acts xix.1-7.

"We have not so much as heard whether there be any Holy Ghost."

Such was the amazing admission of these Ephesian disciples made in response to the Apostle's pointed question, *"Have ye received the Holy Ghost since ye believed?"* At least three remarkable outpourings of the Holy Spirit had taken place since the days of John the Baptist under whose ministry they had been baptised. Within a comparatively short time the great Pentecostal outpouring had stirred the city of Jerusalem from centre to circumference, the more recent revival of signs and wonders at Samaria had been crowned with an outpouring, and since then the Holy Spirit had fallen upon the household of Cornelius at Caesarea. More astonishing still is the confession of the disciples, when we know that John himself had preached the baptism of the Holy Spirit. In the light of these facts it is difficult to understand how they could have been ignorant of the personality and work of the third Person of the Trinity. Yet we who minister in our own privileged land know by experience that such is possible. We are continually coming into contact with professing Christians who do not even know that it is possible to enjoy the assurance of salvation, and, as for the work of the Holy Spirit, multitudes have openly confessed to have been as uninformed as the Ephesian disciples.

In the last chapter we saw the difference between the Spirit of Christ and the Holy Spirit. Certain teachers who have not seen this distinction declare emphatically that it is impossible to be regenerated and not have the Holy Spirit abiding within. The explanation of the Scripture we are now considering is furnished by some of them thus: *"These disciples had been baptised as followers of John the Baptist, not as followers of Christ. The Apostle, discerning their true condition, as unregenerate, wisely presented the Gospel to them in this form, 'Have ye received the Holy Ghost since ye believed?'"*

It would be well for us to examine the Scripture carefully, and to weigh up the evidence in order to discover the true condition of these disciples before they received the Holy Ghost. If we can prove from the Word that there was an interval between the time of their regeneration and their receiving the Holy Ghost, the force of the above argument is destroyed.

Five things are said with regard to them:—

(1) They were disciples.
(2) They had believed.
(3) They had been baptised unto John's baptism.
(4) They were baptised in the name of the Lord Jesus.
(5) They received the Holy Ghost when hands were laid upon them.

This is exactly the order in which they are given. Admitting that disciples (which we know means followers) could be unregenerate, one cannot possibly admit the same of believing disciples. These believing disciples had been baptised unto John's baptism, and in the name of the Lord Jesus Christ. All this before the laying on of hands for the reception of the Holy Ghost is mentioned.

To maintain the idea that they were not regenerated until the Holy Ghost came upon them, one must conclude that those officiating at their baptismal service immersed un-regenerate disciples. Let us, at this juncture, endeavour to find what is meant by the term, "*John's baptism.*" In order to do this, we will consider the message that John preached and the conditions imposed upon those who, having accepted his message, passed through water baptism.

The salient points in his message were:

(1) Warning people to flee from the wrath to come.
(2) Exhorting people to bring forth fruits meet for repentance.
(3) Pointing people to Christ as the Sin-Bearer.
(4) Commanding people to be baptised in water.
(5) Promising through Christ the baptism of the Holy Ghost.

When we read the Acts of the Apostles carefully, we find that these were the salient points in the messages of the Apostles. If this be correct, and we believe it to be so, the Gospel that John preached was the identical Gospel proclaimed by them. Furthermore it is the same Gospel that is entrusted to every true preacher who will abide in the Apostles' doctrine. The difference between John the Baptist and the Apostles was that of position only. John pointed forward, whereas the Apostles pointed backward, to the crucified Christ.

The warning note concerning the wrath of God, sounded by John the Baptist, was as perspicuous as any like note in the Acts of the Apostles. He was fearless in his denunciations as he reminded his congregation of the dark cloud of Jehovah's wrath that must eventually burst over rejecters of the truth. His message falling upon the ears of Sadducees and Pharisees, must have caused much commotion. They were seemingly good people, wrapped up in the conspicuous garb of a formal religion! The class, you remember, who came under the woes of

the Master Himself when He described them as whited sepulchres, full within of dead men's bones and uncleanness. The Baptist's command to flee was in the imperative, if they were to escape sore judgment.

In his exhortation to repentance he was as determined as Peter on the day of Pentecost, and as resolute as Paul on Mars Hill. Repentance to him meant all that the term means. It involved not only feeling sorry, losing tears, and bewailing the fact of past transgressions. It might include all that, but it was incomplete unless accompanied by action on the part of the penitents: "*Bringing forth fruits meet for repentance.*" Behind the flowing robes was the heart that needed cleansing. Long prayers and fasts were no sure evidence of real piety or of true repentance. All the ground is taken from under their feet. They were not allowed to stand even in the merits of Abraham their father. "*Repent!*" was the trumpet note of this wilderness preacher. If the baptism of John meant anything at all, it meant an intelligent acceptance of God's way of salvation by those who, having confessed their sins and repented, were baptised.

It would be most unreasonable to suppose that John baptised unregenerate disciples. Let us turn in this connection to Acts xviii.24,25: *And a certain Jew named Apollos, born at Alexandria, an eloquent man, and mighty in the Scriptures, came to Ephesus. This man was instructed in the way of the Lord; and being fervent in the spirit, he spake and taught diligently the things of the Lord, knowing only the baptism of John.*

Apollos, knowing only the baptism of John, was eloquent and mighty in the Scriptures. He was fervent in spirit and instructed in the way of the Lord, teaching and thus imparting to others the things pertaining to the spiritual realm. Was he a regenerate preacher? It would be difficult to find a reasonable person to affirm that he was not. Unregenerate preachers are not instructed in the way of the Lord. They must first of all enter into the Way, through the door of the new birth, before they can take their places even in the infants' class in God's school of instruction. Paul tells us in 1Corinthians ii.11,14, that a person must possess the Spirit of God before he can understand His things. "*For what man knoweth the things of a man, save the spirit of man which is in him? Even so the things of God knoweth no man, but the Spirit of God... The natural man receiveth not the things of the Spirit of God."*

In Apollos we have a preacher who gave unmistakable evidence of his own regenerated heart. He must have passed through the door into the spiritual realm in order to have such a grasp of its realities. He was emboldened by the Spirit to teach with all diligence the things he must have learned himself. His eloquent preaching, combined with fervency of spirit, supported by his deeply sanctified spiritual life, had appealed to his hearers. Would to God we had preachers like him today! A superabundance of eloquence, rhetoric, and logic will not suffice to reach and convince the masses, unless blended with other characteristics so prominent in the life and ministry of Apollos.

An empowered ministry is the need of our day, without such it is impossible to meet the challenge put forth by the science of the twentieth century. Again, such a ministry alone can deal effectively with the spirit of retrogression found in the present-day churches and missions.

Apollos, like the disciples of Acts xix. knew only the baptism of John. He, like them, had gone on as far as he was able to understand the import of John's message. There was much more land to be possessed by him. There were higher heights to be attained, fresh revelations to be sought, and still deeper experiences through which he was destined to pass, —but he had already possessed the one thing needful: regeneration by the Holy Spirit— before he could explore further afield in the way of God. The pathway of spiritual blessings and experiences was further opened up to him by

Aquila and Priscilla. What did they instruct him in? Did he, under their loving tuition, discover the truth concerning the baptism of the Holy Ghost? Was he led into the experience in a similar way to the disciples of Acts xix? In the spiritual seminary of Aquila and Priscilla we can well imagine the subject of the baptism of the Holy Ghost being the first item on the programme for discussion. We should not be at all surprised if such experienced monitors put the question to him, *"Have ye received the Holy Ghost since ye believed?"* Undoubtedly it was pointed out to him that it was the next step for him to take in the believer's pathway. There may be many of our readers who, having passed into the Kingdom, need a little further instruction along these lines. You might be fervent in the Spirit. You might be able to expound the Scriptures. You have wielded the sword of the Spirit fearlessly in the face of the most bitter opposition of the enemy. You have led many a weeping penitent to the foot of the Cross, and have brought comfort and blessing to many a suffering one. Still, it is our duty to ask you, *"Have ye received the Holy Ghost since ye believed?"* We could call hundreds, if necessary, who would give testimony to the fact that they had all these experiences before they received the Holy Ghost.

The ignorance that prevails concerning the great gift of the Holy Ghost is appalling. In our travels up and down the land, in Scandinavia, Canada and America, we have come across most earnest Christians who have, with astonishment, confessed, *"We have never heard about the baptism of the Holy Ghost in this way before."* The Holy Spirit had often been depicted to them as some mysterious influence, settling or resting upon church congregations in answer to the minister's prayer. The truth of a deep, real, experimental baptism for believers in this age was far beyond their conception. It seemed almost incredible that Christians of today could claim the like gift received by the disciples at Pentecost. The news came to them as a new revelation from God. Many a time have we been present when such received the baptism. The joyous notes of praise proceeding from them have enraptured the soul.

At the commencement of this chapter, we drew your attention to an interpretation of Acts xix.1-6, as given by some teachers. In the latter part of it we are given to understand that the Apostle's discernment of the lack of spirituality in these Ephesian disciples prompted him to put the Gospel to them in this fashion, *"Have ye received the Holy Ghost since ye believed?"* If we are to accept this view, we would have to conclude that Paul, discerning their unregenerate state, asked them if they had received what was impossible for them to receive, being unsaved disciples. The Holy Spirit is God's gift to believers. He is never promised to unbelievers. Our Lord, speaking of the Holy Spirit in John xiv. 16, 17, settles this question once and for all. *"If ye love Me, keep My commandments, and I will pray the Father, and He shall give you another Comforter, that He may abide with you for ever; even the Spirit of Truth; whom the world cannot receive, because it seeth Him not, neither knoweth Him."* We say again that if these Ephesians were unregenerate, they were of the world, and, as such, needed the essential qualification—the new birth—before they could become recipients of the Holy Spirit. We are persuaded that Paul, the scholarly saint, was incapable of making the huge mistake of presenting the Gospel to the unsaved in words that were impossible for them, being carnal, to understand. Paul recognised them as believers and knew that they were qualified to receive the further experience of the baptism in the Holy Ghost.

Let us for a few minutes further consider Paul's usual method of presenting the Gospel to sinners. At Antioch we find him declaring the truth with great authority, and after bringing conviction to bear upon the people, presenting the Gospel to them. *"Be it known unto you therefore, men and brethren, that through this Man is preached unto you the forgiveness of sins."*

We come to Athens, that grand but idolatrous city, where men of mighty intellectual power lay prostrate before gods of wood and stone. Paul is stirred within because of the sins of the people. He is emboldened to preach and declares that God will judge the world in righteousness, by that Man whom He hath ordained. Let us follow in the trail of the Apostles until we find ourselves in the jail at Philippi; Paul and Silas are there, firmly fastened in the stocks. They are in the inner prison, with hands and feet securely fixed. The time passes by and they bear their sufferings patiently, not a murmur or a groan is heard. It is now midnight and full time for family worship. Paul whispers to Silas, *"Let us have one of the Foursquare choruses,"* and they begin to sing praises to God. We do not know what was the actual chorus sung. It might have been *"There is power, power, wonder-working power, in the Blood of the Lamb."* The other prisoners are amazed, and would consider them the most extraordinary of all prisoners. What a difference there was between listening to heart-rending groans, the usual thing in the prison, and these lively choruses. But there are still greater things in store for them. The power of God descends, and the Apostles are shaken so mightily that they are freed from the stocks. *"And suddenly there was a great earthquake, so that the foundations of the prison were shaken, and immediately all the doors were opened, and everyone's bands were loosed."* If ever there was a Pentecostal meeting, it was there. Such a manifestation of power brought conviction upon the gaoler resulting in his cry of distress, *"Sirs! what must I do to be saved?"* We cannot imagine Paul answering by saying, *"Have ye received the Holy Ghost since ye believed?"*

The jailer being a sinner, like those at Antioch and Athens, was introduced to the Saviour. *"Believe on the Lord Jesus Christ, and thou shalt be saved."* The Ephesian disciples being believers, were introduced by Paul to the Holy Ghost, with whom they could be empowered for service in the Christian life.

Chapter 6. Three Baptisms Of The New Testament.

Distinctive in Time; Mode; Experience.
We have proved by experience that the assertion of at least three different baptisms for believers in the New Testament comes to some Bible students with much surprise. Yet by rightly dividing the Word of truth, the fact of these distinct baptisms is clearly demonstrated. Let us look at the Scripture for each separate baptism.
Baptism in the likeness of His death.
Know ye not, that so many of us as were baptised into Jesus Christ were baptised into His death? Therefore we are buried with Him by baptism into death: that like as Christ was raised up from the dead by the glory of the Father, even so we also should walk in newness of life. For if we have been planted together in the likeness of His death, we shall be also in the likeness of His resurrection. Rom.vi,3-5.
Buried with Him in baptism, wherein also ye are risen with Him through the faith of the operation of God who hath raised Him from the dead. Col.ii.12.
Baptism in Water.
Then Philip opened his mouth, and began at the same scripture, and preached unto him Jesus. And as they went on their way, they came unto a certain water: and the eunuch said, See, here is water: what doth hinder me to be baptised? And Philip said, If thou believest with all thine heart, thou mayest. And he answered and said, I believe that Jesus Christ is the Son of God. And he commanded the chariot to stand still: and they went down both into the water, both Philip and the eunuch; and he baptised him. And when they were come up out of the water, the Spirit of

the Lord caught away Philip, that the eunuch saw him no more: and he went on his way rejoicing. Acts viii.35-39.

Baptism with the Holy Spirit.

The next day John seeth Jesus coming unto him, and saith, Behold the Lamb of God, which taketh away the sin of the world... And John bare record, saying, I saw the Spirit descending from heaven like a dove, and it abode upon Him. And I knew Him not: but He that sent me to baptise with water, the same said unto me, upon whom thou shalt see the Spirit descending, and remaining on him, the same is He which baptiseth with the Holy Ghost. John i.29-33.

A careful examination of these Scriptures and their contexts will reveal the distinctive characteristics of each.

Baptism In The Likeness Of His Death.
This baptism must necessarily precede the believer's baptism by immersion in water or else the ordinance would be void of any spiritual significance. It is a deep spiritual experience of identification with Christ in death, and here in Romans vi, it is held forth as an incentive to holy living.

We now proceed to show that this baptism in the likeness of the death of Christ is the immediate normal experience of a person when justified—that it is identical with justification. The question under consideration by the Apostle is that of holiness of life—"*Shall we continue in sin that grace may abound? God forbid.*" He is showing that the habitual life of sin is not consistent with salvation by grace. Evidently there were some believers who held the view, that as their standing before God was made secure through grace, practical holiness did not matter. Such an attitude of mind towards the Kingdom of God received severe condemnation from the Apostle. These people must understand, once and for all, that identification with Christ in death means identification with Him in newness of life. Therefore he takes them back to the place where that new life started, and reminds them of the profession they had made. Had they not been delivered from the old life when they were openly identified with Christ in death at the Cross?

Why then should they seek to continue in that life? Had they not professed to have been immediately raised in newness of life? Why then should they walk in the ways of the old? The Apostle was determined that they should clearly understand that the moment of their justification through the death and resurrection of Christ was the moment of death to the old, and that henceforth they should walk in newness of life.

For if we have been planted together in the likeness of His death, we shall be also in the likeness of His resurrection. Rom.vi.5.

It is evident from the connection between the fifth and sixth chapters of Romans that the baptism in the likeness of the death of Christ, which means deliverance from the old life, is identical with justification. The inspired logician, dealing with the subject of justification in the previous chapters, carries his argument to its logical conclusion in chapter six. Let us see the trend of this argument on Justification.

Justification In Romans V.

Therefore being justified by faith, we have peace with God through our Lord Jesus Christ. Verse 1.

Much more then, being now justified by His blood, we shall be saved from wrath through Him. For if, when we were enemies, we were reconciled to God by the death of His Son, much more, being reconciled, we shall be saved by His life. Verses 9,10

Therefore as by the offence of one judgment came upon all men to condemnation; even so by the righteousness of One the free gift came upon all men unto justification of life. For as By one man's disobedience many were made sinners, so by the obedience of One shall many be made righteous. Moreover the law entered, that the offence might abound. But where sin abounded, grace did much more abound: That as sin hath reigned unto death, even so might grace reign through righteousness unto eternal life by Jesus Christ our Lord. Verses 18-21.

What Shall We Say Then?

Shall we continue in sin, that grace may abound? Rom.vi.1. The Apostle's exclamation in this interrogative form clearly identifies and connects the functioning of justification in chapter five with that of the baptism in the likeness of the death of Christ at the commencement of chapter six.

Baptism By Immersion In Water.

In the Divine order this second baptism should follow on immediately after the baptism in the likeness of the death of Christ. Baptism by immersion gives a clear and distinct testimony to the death and resurrection of Christ, and also to the believer's identification with Him. Alas! this great ordinance has been corrupted in the apostasy of the professing Church, until the fallacy of infant sprinkling has obscured its glorious significance. Others have disregarded the Divine order, and made water baptism the door into Church or Kingdom, and so silenced its powerful message.

Christ outlines the Divine order—Teach, make disciples, then baptize.

And Jesus came and spake unto them, saying, All power is given unto Me in heaven and in earth. Go ye therefore, and teach all nations, baptising them in the Name of the Father, and of the Son, and of the Holy Ghost: Teaching them to observe all things whatsoever I have commanded you: and, lo, I am with you alway, even unto the end of the world. Amen. Matt.xxviii.18-20.

Peter at Pentecost emphasises the order.

Then Peter said unto them, Repent, and be baptised every one of you in the Name of Jesus Christ for the remission of sins... Acts ii.38.

Baptism immediately followed.

Then they that gladly received his word were baptised: and

the same day there were added unto them about three thousand souls. Acts ii.41.
Baptism immediately followed at Samaria.
But when they believed Philip preaching the things concerning the kingdom of God, and the Name of Jesus Christ, they were baptised, both men and women. Acts viii.12.
Baptism immediately followed the Ethiopian's faith.
And as they went on their way, they came unto a certain water: and the eunuch said, See, here is water; what doth hinder me to be baptised? And Philip said, If thou believest with all thine heart, thou mayest... And they went down both into the water... and he baptised him. Acts viii.36-38.

The Mode Of Water Baptism.
There was *"much water"* where John baptised.
And John also was baptising in Ænon near to Salim, because there was much water there: and they came, and were baptised. John iii.23.
Christ baptised in the River Jordan.
And it came to pass in those days, that Jesus came from Nazareth of Galilee, and was baptised of John in Jordan. And straightway coming up out of the water, he saw the heavens opened, and the Spirit like a dove descending upon Him. Mark i.9,10.
The Ethiopian went down and came up.
...And they went down both into the water, both Philip and the eunuch; and he baptised him. And when they were come up out of the water, the Spirit of the Lord caught away Philip, that the eunuch saw him no more: and he went on his way rejoicing. Acts viii.38,39,
Baptism symbolises death, burial, and resurrection, and when applied to the sprinkling of unconscious infants has no meaning at all. But when applied to the

immersion of believers who have, through the exercise of faith, been identified with their Lord in spiritual death and resurrection, it is full of meaning and significance. In the light of these clear statements of Scripture it is amazing to find some Christians who consider this ordinance as unimportant and unessential, and view the matter with indifference whether the sprinkling of infants or the immersion of believers is practised. The same good people would be greatly shocked if they came into contact with those who treated the Lord's Supper in the same way. Yet He who said, "*Do this in remembrance of Me,*" also said, "*Go ye into all the world and preach the Gospel to every creature.*

He that believeth and is baptised shall be saved." The spiritual grace pictured in the ordinance of
Baptism, like that in the Lord's Supper, cannot possibly function upon unconscious babes, but only upon persons who have intelligently accepted eternal life through the death which is symbolised by the ordinance. Neither ordinance is essential to salvation, but both are positive commands to those who are saved. It is most daring and presumptuous of men to set aside the ordinance of Baptism by immersion—which, like the ordinance of the Lord's Supper, Christ Himself instituted—and to substitute another which entirely obscures its original meaning both as to subjects and mode. In this connection Professor Lange, the author of a history of
Protestantism, gives a most consistent view. "*If the Protestant Church would fulfil and attain to its final destiny, the baptism of new-born children must be abolished. It has sunk down to a mere formality, without any religious meaning for the child, and stands in contradiction to the funda-*

mental doctrine of the Reformers on the advantage and use of the Sacraments. It cannot on any point of view be justified by Scripture."

Some of the most profound spiritual analogies in the New Testament are closely related to the truth of baptism by immersion. This ordinance, as practised by the Apostles, stands out through the centuries as an impregnable rock amidst the ever-changing seas of modernistic theory. It solidly withstands the raging billows of twentieth-century Higher Criticism, for it openly testifies to the atoning death and bodily resurrection from the dead of Jesus Christ for our justification. Our Lord was not sprinkled with death as symbolised by traditional infant-sprinkling, but He was immersed in death as symbolised in the Scriptural mode of baptism by immersion.

The love of Christ towards the sinner is manifested in His atoning death, which breaks the fetters of sin.

The love of the believer towards his Saviour is manifested in his obedience to the Word of God, which breaks the fetters of tradition.

The unmistakable evidence of love is its translation into action.

The Baptism Of The Holy Spirit.

This baptism generally came third in the Divine order, and follows on after the baptism by immersion. Believers throughout the present dispensation have testified to the experience after waiting upon God in prayer. Inspired history testifies to the frequent supernatural gift of speaking in tongues that accompanied the baptism in the days of the Apostles. In our day there are tens of thousands all over the world who have the same testimony, and the number is increasing with amazing rapidity. It would be difficult to find one country in the whole world where the Holy Spirit has not fallen in this manner. From north, south, east and west comes the news of Pentecostal outpourings and its miraculous gifts and signs.

We have had thirty-three nationalities represented in one meeting at our Foursquare Gospel demonstrations at the Royal Albert Hall, London, all bound together by the bond of spiritual fellowship. If sometimes we have not been able to converse freely owing to the language difficulty, we have been able to converse at the throne of the heavenly grace. There the language difficulty disappears, for the Spirit divides severally as He will the miraculous gifts whereby we are linked together in communion with God.

The following Scriptures will show that the baptism of the Holy Spirit generally comes third in the Divine order.

Seen in Peter's message at Pentecost.

Then Peter said unto them, Repent, and be baptised every one of you in the Name of Jesus Christ for the remission of sins, and ye shall receive the gift of the Holy Ghost. Acts ii.38.

The order in this scripture is clear:—

(a) "**Repent**": Baptism in the likeness of His death.

(b) "**Be baptised**": Baptism by immersion in water.

(c) "**Ye shall receive**": Baptism in the Holy Spirit.

Seen again at Samaria.

But when they believed Philip preaching the things concerning the kingdom of God, and the Name of Jesus Christ, they were baptised, both men and women. Acts viii.12.

Then laid they their hands on them, and they received the Holy Ghost. Verse 17.

(a) **They believed**: Baptism in the likeness of His death.
(b) **They were baptised**: Baptism by immersion in water.
(c) **They received**: Baptism in the Holy Spirit.

Seen again at Ephesus.

He said unto them, Have ye received the Holy Ghost since ye believed? And they said, unto him, We have not so much as heard whether there be any Holy Ghost. Acts xix.2.

When they heard this, they were baptised in the Name of the Lord Jesus. Verse 5.

And when Paul had laid his hands upon them, the Holy Ghost came on them; and they spake with tongues and prophesied. Verse 6.

(a) **They had believed**: Baptism in the likeness of His death.
(b) **They were baptised**: Baptism by immersion in water.
(c) **They received**: Baptism in the Holy Spirit.

An Exception To
The Divine Order.
At Caesarea.

When charged by those that were of the circumcision with going to the Gentiles Peter declared that the Spirit of God had definitely led him to do so, and that Cornelius, to whom he was sent, had also received news, through a vision, that Peter was coming to convey the message of salvation.

Who shall tell thee words, whereby thou and all thy house shall be saved. Acts xi. 14.

Peter did preach the words whereby Cornelius and his household were saved, for it is evident that they exercised saving Faith in Christ, and received remission of sins while Peter was preaching. Then, while still listening to Peter, they received the Holy Spirit, for He fell on all of them.

While Peter yet spake these words, the Holy Ghost fell on all them which heard the Word. Acts x.44.

This remarkable event has been repeated several times in our own ministry, for the Holy Spirit has fallen exactly as He did in Cornelius' house, and with the same signs, while words like the following were going forth—*"To Him give all the prophets witness, that through His Name whosoever believeth in Him shall receive remission of sins"* (Acts x. 43).

The Gentiles at the house of Cornelius received the gift of the Holy Spirit before they were baptised in water.

Can any man forbid water, that these should not be baptised, which have received the Holy Ghost as well as we? Verse 47. And he commanded them to be baptised in the Name of the Lord. Then prayed they him to tarry certain days. Verse 48.

(a) **They believed on Christ**: Baptism in the likeness of His death.

(b) **The Holy Ghost fell on them**: Baptism in the Holy Ghost.

(c) **Baptism afterwards commanded**: Baptism by immersion in water.

But God, in His sovereign right, on this occasion, changed the usual order by baptising the household of Cornelius in the Holy Spirit before they were baptised in water, as the quoted scriptures show.

Different Agents At Each Separate Baptism.

The following analysis of these baptisms proves conclusively that they are three distinct acts.

The Divine Agent who operates at the new birth is— The Holy Spirit.
He convicts of sin.
And when He is come, He will reprove the world of sin, and of righteousness, and of judgment. John xvi.8.
He regenerates.
Jesus answered, Verily, verily, I say unto thee, Except a man be born of water, and of the Spirit, he cannot enter into the kingdom of God. John iii.5.
Regeneration is identical with justification, and justification as we have shown, is identical with the baptism in the likeness of the death of Christ.

The agent who officiates at the baptism by immersion in water is— The Minister.
And he commanded the chariot to stand still: and they went down both into the water, both Philip and the eunuch; and he baptised him. Acts viii.38.

The Divine Agent who baptises with the Holy Spirit is— The Lord Jesus Christ.
And John bare record, saying, I saw the Spirit descending from heaven like a dove, and it abode upon Him, And I knew Him not: but He that sent me to baptise with water, the same said unto me, Upon whom thou shalt see the Spirit descending, and remaining on Him, the same is He which baptiseth with the Holy Ghost. John i.32,33.

A Difference In The Subjects.

The subject at the baptism in the likeness of the death of Christ is— The sinner.
For if we have been planted together in the likeness of His death, we shall be also in the likeness of His resurrection. Rom.vi.5.

The subject at the baptism

**by immersion in water is
— The believer.**

And a certain woman named Lydia, a seller of purple, of the city of Thyatira, which worshipped God, heard us: whose heart the Lord opened, that she attended unto the things which were spoken of Paul. And when she was baptised, and her household, she besought us, saying, If ye have judged me to be faithful to the Lord, come into my house, and abide there... Acts xvi.14,15.

**The subject at the baptism of the
Holy Spirit is also— The believer.**

For John truly baptised with water; but ye shall be baptised with the Holy Ghost not many days hence. Acts i.5, He said unto them, Have ye received the Holy Ghost since ye believed? And they said unto him, We have not so much as heard whether there be any Holy Ghost. Acts xix.2.

**Different Elements At Each
Separate Baptism. The element
in the first baptism is—
The death of Christ.**

The sinner must be willing for his old life to go down into death in the person of his Saviour, if he is to experience newness of life in Christ. It is only on this ground that God can justify him, and this is the reason why we point sinners to the Cross. We have already shown that justification is identical with this baptism.

Know ye not, that so many of us as were baptised into Jesus Christ, were baptised into His death? Rom.vi.3.

Buried with Him in baptism, wherein also ye are risen with Him through the faith of the operation of God. Col.ii.12.

**The element in the second baptism is—
Water: in which the officiating minister immerses the believer.**

Can any man forbid water that these should not be baptised...? Acts x.47.

The element in the third baptism is—

The Holy Spirit: in whom the Lord Jesus baptises the believer:

I indeed have baptised you with water: but He [Christ] shall baptise you with the Holy Ghost. Mark i.8.

Baptism In The Likeness Of His Death.	
Agent	**The Holy Spirit.**
Subject	**The Sinner.**
Element	**Death**
Baptism By Immersion In Water.	
Agent	**The Minister.**
Subject	**The Believer.**
Element	**Water.**
Baptism With The Holy Spirit.	
Agent	**The Lord Jesus.**
Subject	**The Believer.**
Element	**The Holy Spirit.**

Chapter 7. Three Baptisms In Type.

An Old Testament Word Picture
So he [Elijah] departed thence, and found Elisha... who was plowing with twelve yoke of oxen before him... and Elijah passed by him, and cast his mantle upon him... Then he arose, and went after Elijah. 1Kings xix.19,21. And Elijah took his mantle and... smote the waters and... they two went over on dry ground. 2Kings ii.8. He took up also the mantle of Elijah that fell from him. 2Kings ii.13.

To all who are acquainted with their foreshadowing truths Old Testament types stand out with grandeur of conception and minuteness of detail. No human mind could ever imagine anything more edifying and exquisitely beautiful than the truths which are mirrored in the vast arrangement of Old Testament typology. Yet it should be borne in mind that New Testament truth, particularly doctrine, cannot be established by these types. Doctrine is founded on the plain declarations of Scripture, chiefly the Church Epistles, and these must not be explained so as to fit in with any Old Testament picture. The true type must answer to the doctrine, and not the doctrine to the type, if we are rightly to divide the Word of Truth. We have always maintained that it is not a sound method of interpretation to build New Testament truth, particularly doctrine, on types, incidents, or prophecy. We are therefore viewing the call of Elisha from the field, his passing through the Jordan, and his equipment for service, as a type, because it corresponds with the teaching of the New Testament.

The believer's separation from his former life answers to Elisha's separation from his former life as antitype to type. The believer passing through the waters of baptism answers to Elisha passing through the river Jordan. The believer receiving an equipment for service answers to Elisha receiving the mantle of Elijah.

In this Old Testament word picture we see Elijah the prophet clothed with a mantle that hangs loosely upon his shoulders. In the background of the picture is the field, and in the field a ploughman named Elisha, ploughing with twelve yoke of oxen. As we meditate, the picture begins to live, for the prophet wends his way towards the field in the distance, and when it is reached he touches the ploughman with his mantle and makes him his disciple. Elisha becomes the follower of the great prophet, and after passing through various experiences, including his passage through the Jordan, he receives as a gift the mantle that had touched him when in the field of former days.

Type And Antitype.
The Prophet: a type of the Saviour.
The Mantle: a type of the Holy Spirit. **The Ploughman**: a type of the Sinner. **The Field**: a type of the World.

Elijah the prophet is an outstanding character in Old Testament Scriptures. He was a wonderful man because the God of wonders was with him. Elijah believed in the essentially supernatural element of his religion, and accordingly experienced the miraculous in his ministry. Yet in face of his great works and mighty accomplishments in the name of his God, some of which we enumerate, we are told that he was an ordinary man, subject to like passions as his fellow men.

Elijah locks the heavens.

And Elijah the Tishbite, who was of the inhabitants of Gilead, said unto Ahab, As the Lord God of Israel liveth, before whom I stand, there shall not be dew nor rain these years, but according to my word. 1 Kings xvii.1.

Heavens unlocked three-and-a-half years later.

And Elijah said unto Ahab, get thee up, eat and drink; for there is a sound of abundance of rain... And it came to pass in the meanwhile, that the heaven was black with clouds and wind, and there was a great rain. 1 Kings xviii.41,45.

Elias was a man subject to like passions as we are, and he prayed earnestly that it might not rain: and it rained not on the earth by the space of three years and six months. And he prayed again, and the heaven gave rain, and the earth brought forth her fruit. James v.17,18.

Miraculously fed in time of famine.

And the ravens brought him bread and flesh in the morning, and bread and flesh in the evening; and he drank of the brook. 1 Kings xvii.6.

Multiplied meal and oil.

And she went and did according to the saying of Elijah: and she, and he, and her house, did eat many days. And the barrel of meal wasted not, neither did the cruse of oil fail, according to the word of the Lord, which He spake by Elijah. 1 Kings xvii.15,16.

Raised the dead.

And it came to pass after these things, that the son of the woman, the mistress of the house, fell sick; and his sickness was so sore, that there was no breath left in him. And the Lord heard the voice of Elijah; and the soul of the child came into him again, and he revived. And Elijah took the child, and brought him down out of the chamber into the house, and delivered him unto his mother: and Elijah said, See, thy son liveth. 1 Kings xvii.17,22,23.

Fire descends from heaven.

And it came to pass at the time of the offering of the evening sacrifice, that Elijah the prophet came near, and said, Lord God of Abraham, Isaac, and of Israel, let it be known this day that Thou art God in Israel, and that I am Thy servant, and that I have done all these things at Thy word. Hear me, O Lord, hear me, that this people may know that Thou art the Lord God, and that Thou hast turned their heart back again. Then the fire of the Lord fell, and consumed the burnt sacrifice, and the wood, and the stones, and the dust, and licked up the water that was in the trench. And when all the people saw it, they fell on their faces: and they said, The Lord, He is the God; the Lord, He is the God. 1 Kings xviii.36-39.

God's Friends.

Combined with Elijah's faithful service was the close intimacy, that worshipful communion and sweet fellowship that mark him out as God's friend, like Abraham, and as His companion, like Enoch. These three characters in the Old Testament were destined to stand out conspicuously throughout future dispensations as examples to all believers. It would not surprise us if we were told that Elijah was definitely informed beforehand of his translation to be with his God. The revelation might easily have been given during one of those heart-to-heart talks together. We are definitely told that Elijah before he was caught up called Elisha from the plough to the service of God. It was evidently part of the plan for Elisha to become his successor in the prophet's office. God's way of calling to a service so important is very unlike man's way. If the choice had been left to an ecclesiastical council consideration might only be given to applicants with tall foreheads, blue blood in the veins, or with letters to their names. Not so with God, as we see in the following appointments:—

Moses called to be law-giver and statesman.

Now Moses kept the flock of Jethro his father-in-law, the priest of Midian: and he led the flock to the backside of the desert, and came to the mountain of God, even to Horeb. Now therefore, behold, the cry of the children of Israel is come unto Me: and I have also seen the oppression wherewith the Egyptians oppress them. Come now therefore, and I will send thee unto Pharaoh, that thou mayest bring forth My people the children of Israel out of Egypt. Ex.iii.1,9,10.

Gideon called to be field marshal.

And the Lord looked upon him, and said, Go in this thy might, and thou shalt save Israel from the hand of the Midianites: have not I sent thee? And he said unto him, Oh my Lord, wherewith shall I save Israel? behold, my family is poor in Manasseh, and I am the least in my father's house. And the Lord said unto him, Surely I will be with thee, and thou shalt smite the Midianites as one man. Judges vi.14-16.

David called to be king.

And Samuel said unto Jesse, Are here all thy children? And he said, There remaineth yet the youngest, and, behold, he keepeth the sheep. And Samuel said unto Jesse, Send and fetch him: for we will not sit down till he come hither... Then Samuel took the horn of oil, and anointed him in the midst of his brethren: and the Spirit of the Lord came upon David from that day forward. 1Sam.xvi.11-13.

Let us now consider the typical import of the narrative before us.

Type And Antitype.
Type - Elisha leaves the field to follow Elijah.
And he left the oxen, and ran after Elijah... and ministered unto him. 1Kings xix.20,21.
Antitype - Disciples leave the world to follow Christ.
And he said unto them, Unto what then were ye baptized? And they said, Unto John's baptism. Then said Paul, John verily baptised with the baptism of repentance, saying unto the people, that they should believe on Him which should come after him, that is, on Christ Jesus. Acts xix.3,4.

The touch of Elijah's mantle resulted in the ploughman breaking up his wooden ploughs, and bidding farewell to the field and his acquaintances. Something had happened in his experience that day that meant dying to the old and living in the new. The field could no longer hold him, for contact with Elijah had created an urge within to follow the prophet. It was the beginning of days for him, for he began to live in a new world. He was planted in the likeness of death to the past life, and resurrected to a new life in the future.

It was the same with the Ephesian disciples whom Elisha typifies. They had repented, and had turned from the world to follow Christ, as they were taught by John the Baptist. The regenerating touch of the Saviour meant to them the breaking up of old acquaintances, the destruction of sinful habits and separation from the world. Regeneration had created an urge within to leave the old paths and follow the new. They were planted in the likeness of Christ's death, and were raised in newness of life; and this life called for a new walk, new pleasures, and new companions. Until the sinner accepts Christ as Saviour, he merely exists, even though he may be extremely religious; but the moment he comes into contact with Him he begins to live. Elisha having left, the field is called to go through a series of tests as the 2nd chapter of the 2nd book of Kings shows. *"Tarry here, I pray thee, for the Lord hath sent me to Bethel,"* said Elijah, giving Elisha an opportunity to cease following. But the answer is soon given, *As the Lord liveth and as thy soul liveth, I will not leave thee."* Bethel is reached and the second time the disciple is tested, *"Elisha, tarry here, I pray thee, for the Lord hath sent me to Jericho,"* and again the reply is the same. Jericho is reached, and for the third and last test the way that leads to Jordan is chosen by the disciple rather than retirement at Jericho— *"And they two went on."*

Elisha had learned to trust his master under all kinds of circumstances, and when he decides to follow he is assured of his presence with him. How encouraging the words of our Lord are to His disciples— *"I will never leave thee."*

The disciple can trust the One who through the touch of regeneration caused him to leave the world of sin, to break up the old associations, and to leave all, for he is assured that he will never be forsaken by his Lord.

Jordan is reached, and Elisha is to witness the great miracle of the dividing of the waters.

Type - Through the waters with Elijah.
And Elijah took his mantle, and wrapped it together, and smote the waters, and they were divided hither and thither, so that they two went over on dry ground. 2 Kings ii.8.
Antitype - Through the waters with Christ.
When they heard this, they were baptised in the name of the Lord Jesus. Acts xix. 5.

The mantle that had separated Elisha from the field now makes a unique baptismal font right in the heart of Jordan. The waters miraculously divided hither and thither are walled up on both sides. The pathway is ready and soon Elisha follows Elijah into that which mirrored the baptism of believers in the New Testament. They went down to the bed of Jordan, walked right through, and came up again the other side.

Here the disciple is seen passing through the same waters as his Master. What a beautiful picture of those Ephesian disciples who, having believed on the Lord Jesus Christ, followed Him through the waters of baptism.

Elisha having passed typically from death into life when touched by the mantle in the field, having also passed through the typical waters of baptism, is about to experience a third baptism in type—the baptism of the Holy Spirit. The day of Elijah's translation to heaven came, and the revelation is made known to the disciple. Elisha chose the proffered parting gift, *"Let a double portion of thy Spirit be upon* me," and they both went on together. Then the heavens are opened, and in the distance is seen the flaming chariot. It comes nearer and nearer until the sand of the desert is disturbed, and when near enough Elijah steps into the chariot and is taken heavenward. Then as the flaming chariot with its privileged passenger ascends, the silence of the desert is broken by the clear ringing notes of the lone disciple. *"My father, my father, the chariot of Israel, and the horsemen thereof."* The Scripture says, *"he cried"*—it was no whispering undertone: Elisha, the disciple, rent the air with his cries until they reached the ears of the departing prophet. If any of the conservative sons of the prophet were near enough we feel sure they would have tried to restrain the enthusiast. They would have advised him to say the words quietly, that there was no need for such a noise, and not to be so emotional. But to Elisha the occasion demanded wholehearted surrender of all he possessed, even his vocal organs to praise the God of Israel while waiting for the mantle. Sanctified emotion did not seem out of place to one who had received the promise of power for service. His master was departing, and it behoved him to be full-throated as well as full-hearted in his quest of the desired blessing.

How often have we met religious people in our day who regard all audible praise as mere emotion. It is not to be wondered at that they do not experience revival, for there can be no revival without the sanctified praises of God's people. Why such folk consider praise and ejaculations during times of revival as noise is because their hearts are not tuned in to heaven. If they were, the cries of the penitent, and the singing of the loud and full-throated praises of the redeemed, would fall upon their ears as the most exquisite harmony.

The departing prophet must have been tuned in to the cries of Elisha, for it was not long until the answer came

—

Type - The mantle of power descends.
He took up also the mantle of Elijah that fell from him, and went back, and stood by the bank of Jordan. 2 Kings ii.13.
Antitype - The Holy Spirit descends.
And when Paul had laid his hands upon them, the Holy Ghost came on them, and they spake with tongues, and prophesied. Acts xix.6.

The mantle that had brought Elisha into newness of life when in the field, and had made the passage through the waters of Jordan possible, now clothed him with power. The antitype in the 19th chapter of the Acts of the Apostles also reveals the order in which the Ephesian disciples received the Holy Spirit. Firstly, they were convicted of their sins by the Holy Spirit, and had left the world to follow Christ, whom John the Baptist preached. Secondly, they followed in the footsteps of their Lord, for they were baptised in His Name. Thirdly, the Holy Spirit came upon them as the Apostle laid his hands upon them.

Elisha in the desert was alone, yet not alone, for he possessed the very mantle which had so mightily clothed- Elijah. True, his master had gone, but he possessed his power. Elisha is to be pardoned if he was anxious to put the mantle to immediate test, for it is not long until he stands at the bank of Jordan. If the religious sons of the prophets had met him before he reached the bank they might have argued with him thus, "*It is no use exercising yourself, Elisha, for the supernatural power was withdrawn when your master ascended. You must join us now, and like us live in the higher plane of faith without signs or miracles. The supernatural element was necessary in the days of Elijah, when he had to contend with the mighty Ahab, but now that we are living in a different and more enlightened dispensation it is quite unnecessary.*"

But all the arguments that the sons of the prophets might raise were doomed to fall before the demonstration that followed. Elisha, clothed with the same mantle, smote the waters of Jordan, and they were walled up again as they were in the days of Elijah—

And he took the mantle of Elijah that fell from him, and smote the waters, and said, Where is the Lord God of Elijah? and when he also had smitten the waters, they parted hither and thither... 2 Kings ii.14.

The disciples mentioned in the Acts received an

equipment for service when the Holy Spirit came upon them, and, as with the disciples at Pentecost, the Spirit took possession of their vocal organs, and they spoke with tongues and also prophesied. They had been baptised into the death of Christ when they in faith accepted the Lamb of God who had come to take away their sins.

Like Isaiah the prophet they could say, "*The Lord hath laid on Him the iniquity of us all.*" They experienced the second baptism when they went through the waters in the name of the Lord Jesus. The third baptism which these Ephesian disciples experienced was that of the Holy Spirit. Like Elisha they had received power for service from the One who had made them disciples. The Master had departed, but His power remained!

Chapter 8. The Relations Of The Holy Spirit To Christ's Human Nature And His Relations To Every Believer.

The Spirit of the Lord is upon Me, because He hath anointed Me to preach the gospel to the poor: He hath sent Me to heal the broken-hearted, to preach deliverance to the captives, and recovering of sight to the blind, to set at liberty them that are bruised, to preach the acceptable year of the Lord. Luke iv.18-19.
But ye shall receive power, after that the Holy Ghost is come upon you: and ye shall be witnesses unto Me both in Jerusalem, and in all Judea, and in Samaria, and unto the uttermost part of the earth. Acts i.8.

In this chapter we propose considering the work undertaken by the Holy Spirit in the great scheme of redemption. Let us go back in imagination to a scene in eternity. There, sitting in council, is the Trinity, Father, Son and Holy Ghost, deliberating upon a theme of profound interest. The future course of the ages is scanned by the omniscient Mind, and a distant scene reveals the fall of the greatest and mightiest of all created beings. Redeeming love, finding its source in the heart of God, rolls on, carrying in its train the gift of an essential, redeeming Sacrifice. The Trinity was indeed concerned in the plan of redemption. Each a separate personality, having mutual relations to the others, had His distinctive work to do.

God The Father Gave His Son,
For God so loved the world, that He gave His only begotten Son, that whosoever believeth in Him should not perish, but

have everlasting life. John iii.16.

Jesus The Son Volunteered To Come.

Therefore doth My Father love Me, because I lay down My life, that I might take it again. No man taketh it from Me, but I lay it down of Myself. I have power to lay it down, and I have power to take it again. This commandment have I received of My Father. John x.17,18.

The Holy Ghost Prepared The Way.

Wherefore when He [Christ] cometh into the world, He saith, Sacrifice and offering Thou wouldest not, but a body hast Thou [the Holy Ghost] prepared Me. Heb.x.5.

The body in which the Second Person of the Trinity dwelt was prepared and fitted by its Author, the Third Person of the Trinity; for—

Jesus Was Born Of The Holy Spirit.

And the angel answered and said unto her, The Holy Ghost shall come upon thee, and the power of the Highest shall overshadow thee; therefore also that holy thing which shall be born of thee, shall be called the Son of God. Luke i.35.

This brings us to our first proposition in a most striking analogy between the relations of the Holy Ghost to the human nature of Christ, and His relations to all regenerated souls. Christ's human nature was prepared and fitted by the Holy Spirit, as a temple through which the Deity could be made manifest. These are days when the virgin birth is discredited by some religious teachers who carry indisputable marks of latter-day apostasy. The real Man, Jesus, born of a human mother and begotten of the Holy Ghost, is a fact that cannot be acknowledged by them because of their carnal and darkened minds. Little, if at all, do they understand the things pertaining to the Spirit.

In Bethlehem's manger we see the human temple

made by the Holy Ghost to conceal the glory of the Son of God from the eyes of sinful men. Here lies the body that possessed all the appetites and propensities of human nature, and which was destined to reach the culminating point in a life of victory over the world, the flesh, and the Devil. Here we find the veil that hid in its folds the One who was the brightness of His Father's glory. Having stepped into a little world of flesh, He set His face steadfastly towards Jerusalem, where at the appointed time, He could, by its rending, open up a new and living way into His Father's presence.

The Holy Spirit who was the author of the human nature of Christ, is also the author of the new creation in Christ Jesus.

True Christians are born of the Holy Spirit.

As many as received Him, to them gave He power to become the sons of God, even to them that believe on His name : which were born, not of blood, nor of the will of the flesh, nor of the will of man, but of God. John i.12,13.

That which is born of the Spirit is spirit. John iii.6.

The Holy Spirit, operating at the new birth, is continually seeking human temples for God to dwell in. He convicts of sin, and when the sinner turns to God, and exercises faith in Christ, He works the great miracle of regeneration within. The mortal body, that wonderful organism with its millions of living cells, its astonishing brain, its marvellous faculties of sight, touch, and hearing, becomes an earthen vessel containing heavenly treasure. Through it God is pleased to reveal His life to the world and by it make known His power. It pleases Him to give visible manifestations of His presence, in mortal temples not made with hands, just as real as He did long ago in temples made by the hand of man. In fulfilment of the promise given by Christ to the disciples before Calvary—*"He dwelleth with you, and shall be in you"*— the Holy Spirit took up His abode within each one on the day of Pentecost. Upon those waiting ones the Shekinah descended, and the physical phenomena which accompanied it were the assertion by God of His lordship over the whole being—spirit, soul and body. Wonder of wonders, that the Creator of worlds of whom Solomon said, *"Behold, the heaven of heavens cannot contain Thee,"* condescends to make the saved sinner His dwelling-place.

Jesus Was Sealed With The Holy Spirit.

Now when all the people were baptised, it came to pass that Jesus also being baptised, and praying, the heaven was opened, And the Holy Ghost descended in a bodily shape like a dove upon Him, and a voice came from Heaven, which said, Thou art My beloved Son; in Thee I am well pleased. Luke iii.21,22.

Him hath God the Father sealed. John vi.27.

The manifestation of God in human nature was indeed a mystery, a startling prodigy conceived in the infinite Mind before worlds were made. Christ was hidden in the Old Testament types and shadows, and at last revealed in the manger of a poor innkeeper's stable at Bethlehem. His coming into this realm of nature burst on a dark and God-forsaken age like a bright and glorious day. His appearance here was a step in the pathway leading to a complete and finished work.

The goal in view was the Cross, and its shadow was already thrown upon the crude cradle. Many and varied were the experiences through which this Child was destined to pass before completing the scheme undertaken for the redemption of mankind. It is not possible for us to watch His spotless life or to trace His early footsteps through the sacred page. As the years roll on in silence we can imagine Him, behind the veil of obscurity, attending to His Father's business, and ever pressing forward to the desired goal. In the Scripture first quoted we find Him a full-grown man, about the age of thirty. He is about to commence an unceasing and untiring ministry of a few years' duration, before which He is sealed by God the Father. The

Holy Spirit descended upon Him in bodily shape, like a dove. The Author of His human nature now comes to empower Him for service. His future ministry, with its stupendous display of phenomenal manifestations, was the result of such an equipment. This was another remarkable work of the Holy Spirit which the human Jesus experienced. This reminds us of a Scripture that speaks of saints being sealed subsequently to their regeneration.

Christians can be sealed with the Holy Spirit

In whom ye also trusted, after that ye heard the word of truth, the gospel of your salvation: in whom also, after that ye believed, ye were sealed with that Holy Spirit of promise. Eph.i.13.

The new birth is but the door leading into the Kingdom of God—the gate at the entrance of the spiritual domain, the beauties of which would be impossible to behold, if an entrance had not been gained. Once inside you are invited to step into the symbolical waters of baptism, and give testimony before principalities and powers of your identification with a buried and risen Lord.

The vista of Christian privileges and experiences opens up before you, and in the distance are seen the transcendent heights of spiritual revelation. You become immediately eligible for the fulfilment of the promise of the Father. Like your Master, you can be sealed and equipped for service. The fact that you have become a child and an heir of God, will not relieve you of spiritual conflict. You will have to contend with a real, live, powerful enemy. Indeed, you never come to grips with him, until you come through the gate of regeneration. When you were outside, you were absolutely under his control, you had become his slave, and were powerless to offer the least resistance. But having been emancipated and delivered from him, you will find that he is going to challenge seriously every step you now purpose taking. You need not, however, be discouraged. You were not born of the Spirit to be allowed to die at the hands of a cruel and relentless foe. God has provided an equipment for you, which will ward off his fiery darts, and give you, while passing through the most treacherous and dangerous onslaught, the firm tread of a conqueror every time. Listen! *"Ye shall receive power after that the Holy Ghost is come upon you... Tarry ye in the city of Jerusalem, until ye be endued with power from on high."* It is for you to claim the promises. Go in for a real baptism of the Holy Ghost, which is your birthright as a child of God.

Jesus Acted In The Power Of The Holy Spirit.
God anointed Jesus of Nazareth with the Holy Ghost, and with power: who went about doing good, and healing all that were oppressed of the devil. Acts x.38.
The messengers sent by John the Baptist to the Master witnessed such a demonstration of the power of the Holy Spirit. They had been perplexed by a question that passed through their minds. Is this the One we have

been daily looking for? The answer was soon forthcoming, in the mighty works which He accomplished in their presence. That old man yonder who has been burdened with infirmity for years, immediately receives a new lease of life. The demoniac who struck terror to the hearts of his neighbours by his agonising cries, is sitting at His feet, calm and reposed. That woman who was in the grip of a fearful plague which has swept numbers into untimely graves, is rejoicing because in her case it has been stayed by the word of His mouth.

With astonishment they watch those who have hitherto been blind, as they with open eyes scan the glory of the heavens above and the beauties of nature around. Crutches, carriages, and various implements, having served their purpose, are discarded. The paralysed and the lame need them no longer, for their limbs have been made perfectly whole. Unsightly lepers need no more cry, "*Unclean.*" They, too, have found in Him a balm that has healed their otherwise incurable disease. The deaf hear, the dead are raised, and to the poor the Gospel is preached. All this was sufficient evidence to convince the messengers and John that Jesus was the Anointed One.

Christians should act in the power of the Holy Spirit.

Verily, verily, I say unto you, He that believeth on Me, the works that I do shall he do also and greater works than these shall he do: because I go unto My Father. John xiv.12.

Ye shall receive power, after that the Holy Ghost is come upon you: and ye shall be witnesses unto Me. Acts i.8.

Believers are not only to conform to the pattern of their Lord's spotless life. They are also exhorted to be like Him in the exercise of His power over all the forces of evil. This was evidently in the mind of Christ when He prayed for the disciples. *"As Thou hast sent Me into the world, even so have I also sent them into the world."* His disciples must live like Him, true enough! They must also act like Him! There are real demon-possessed people to be dealt with, there are the sick and afflicted to be ministered to. The sphere in which they live and operate is one dominated by spiritual wickedness in high places. Likened unto ambassadors, they have the authority of the Heavenly Kingdom which they represent. They are not invested with the limited powers of an earthly court, but with unlimited Divine authority. To be effective in their representations before a godless, Christ-rejecting world, they need the Divine credentials which are obtained by the Baptism of the Holy Spirit. If they are to act in the interests of their King and Country, they must be clothed with power from on high.

Jesus Offered Himself Through The Holy Spirit.
For if the blood of bulls, and of goats and the ashes of an heifer sprinkling the unclean, sanctifieth to the purifying of the flesh: How much more shall the blood of Christ, who, through the eternal spirit offered Himself without spot to God, purge your conscience from dead works to serve the living God? Heb.ix,13,14.

If this Scripture means anything, it is that the human Jesus received from the Holy Spirit strength to go to Calvary. The Spirit with whom He was anointed to preach the Gospel to the poor, to heal the broken-hearted, to deliver the captives, to heal the bruised arid give recovery of sight to the blind, was the same who anointed Him to go to the Cross as an Offering for sin.

Who can enter into the feelings of the human Jesus, as He laboured day and night with the shadow of the

Cross upon Him? In His meditation of the Old Testament Scriptures He would be reminded in types and shadows of the humiliating death at the end of life's journey. The pathway that led to the Cross was one of intense suffering. The severity of the onslaught by the powers of darkness to crush the life out of Him before reaching the Cross, called for an anointing such as He received in order to reach His desired goal. Who can tell of the many times He received quickening for His tired and weakened human frame from the Holy Spirit that descended upon Him at the commencement of His public ministry? The Author of His human nature anointed Him and enabled Him to reach the Cross, and there through the eternal Spirit His body was given an offering for sin.

Christians are exhorted to make an offering.
I beseech you therefore, brethren, by the mercies of God, that ye present your bodies a living sacrifice, holy, acceptable unto God, which is your reasonable service. Rom.xii.1.
The offering of the body of Christ to atone for sin was once and for all, and there is no need to offer another for this purpose. But there is need for human channels through which God can manifest Himself to those for whom Christ died. It is evident that the writer to the saints at Rome is meditating upon the offerings of the Old Testament as he writes this Scripture. He is taking lessons from what transpired when the offering was presented, and applying them to the saints of his day. These things stand out prominently as we consider the matter:—

(1) **The utter abandonment of the offering.**
(2) **The incisive priestly knife.**
(3) **The draining of the life blood of the offering.**

The Christian must hand over his body absolutely, without reserve. Presented, never to be withdrawn, he must be willing for his Lord to do with him just what He considers best. Again, he must be willing for the knife to be put in. There are many Christians who are wedded to things which can only be severed by the sharp two-edged sword of the Spirit. Furthermore, once the body is placed at the disposal of God and is ready for service, the life, just like the blood of the Old Testament offering, will flow out. It will become a channel, a living sacrifice, out of which will flow a constant stream of blessing to all around. Through the anointing of the Holy Spirit such an experience is possible to all saints.

Jesus Was Raised From The Dead By The Holy Spirit.
For Christ also hath once suffered for sins, the just for the unjust, that He might bring us to God; being put to death in the flesh, but quickened by the Spirit. 1Pet.iii.18.
Jesus, on the Cross, said, "*It is finished,*" and the sound went back to the past ages of time, declaring that Calvary was the end to which all the Old Testament types and shadows pointed. The darkness of the Crucifixion is over, and the body, which has been offered through the eternal Spirit, has been drained of its life blood. It is carried by a few faithful followers to the proffered sepulchre, there to await another manifestation of Divine power which would crown all others. The sacred temple of flesh which had been conceived, nourished, strengthened, sealed and equipped by the Holy Ghost, is not to be forgotten in the tomb. Old Testament prophecies relating to His miraculous birth, His spotless life, His ignominious death, and even the rich man's tomb, had now been translated into history. His body, which was marred to such an extent that people

were astonished as they gazed upon it, still retained every bone unbroken, according to the Scriptures. But there was a Scripture in a prophetic psalm relating to His resurrection that must be fulfilled: *"For Thou wilt not leave My soul in hell; neither wilt Thou suffer Thine Holy One to see corruption."* The third morning comes, and in order to frustrate, if possible, the fore-ordained plan, we find the tomb sealed and closely guarded. The Holy Spirit, breaking through every hindrance, quickens into life that holy flesh, and raises Him from the dead.

Christians will be raised by the Holy Spirit.

The dead in Christ shall rise first: Then we which are alive and remain shall be caught up together with them in the clouds, to meet the Lord in the air. 1 Thess.iv.16,17.

That ye may know... what is the exceeding greatness of His power to us-ward who believe, according to the working of His mighty power, which He wrought in Christ, when He raised Him from the dead. Eph.i.18-20. Paul, in his Ephesian epistle, is revealing the future relations of the Holy Spirit to believers. He shows that the great work commenced by the Spirit in the bodies of saints would not terminate until they were not only delivered from the power of sin, but from death and the grave. The sealing with the promised Holy Spirit was but the pledge and foretaste of their inheritance. They could look forward, with joyful anticipation, to the full redemption of their bodies. This would be realised, as he declared elsewhere, at the coming of his Lord.

Having thus studied the operations of the Holy Spirit upon the human Jesus, as analogous to the relations of the Spirit to believers, we trust that the work of the Third Person in the Trinity will have been made clearer. The Holy Spirit who brought conviction to bear upon you, dear one, when you were in your sins, also led you to the Cross and revealed the shed blood that was efficacious to cleanse. He who came to abide in your life in answer to prayer, and who led you on step by step, will, at the appointed time, cause mortality to be swallowed up of life.

Chapter 9. Fruit Of The Spirit And The Gifts Of The Holy Spirit.

In a previous chapter we have considered the difference between the Spirit of Christ and the Holy Spirit.[1] We shall now see the difference between the Fruit of the Spirit and the Gifts of the Holy Spirit.

The nine-fold fruit of the Spirit.

But the fruit of the Spirit is love, joy, peace, longsuffering, gentleness, goodness, faith, meekness, temperance: against such there is no law. Gal.v.22,23.

The nine gifts of the Holy Spirit.

But the manifestation of the Spirit is given to every man to profit withal. For to one is given by the Spirit the word of wisdom; to another the word of knowledge by the same Spirit; to another faith by the same Spirit; to another the gifts of healing by the same Spirit; to another the working of miracles; to another prophecy; to another discerning of spirits; to another divers kinds of tongues; to another the interpretation of tongues. 1Cor.xii.7-10.

Let us at this juncture emphasize two facts of vital importance to the subject if we are to get a right perspective:

Firstly, that the Holy Spirit was not given before or during the days of our Lord's earthly ministry.

In the last day, that great day of the feast, Jesus stood and cried, saying, If any man thirst, let him come unto Me, and drink. He that believeth on Me, as the Scripture hath said, out of him shall flow rivers of living water. (But this spake He of the Spirit, which they that believe on Him should receive: for the Holy Ghost was not yet given; because that

Jesus was not yet glorified.) John vii.37-39.

Secondly, that although the Holy Spirit had not been given, the disciples were exhorted to bring forth the fruit of the Spirit in their day.

Abide in Me, and I in you. As the branch cannot bear fruit of itself, except it abide in the vine; no more can ye, except ye abide in Me. I am the vine, ye are the branches: he that abideth in Me, and I in him, the same bringeth forth much fruit: for without Me ye can do nothing... Ye have not chosen Me, but I have chosen you, and ordained you, that ye should go and bring forth fruit, and that your fruit should remain: that whatsoever ye shall ask of the Father in My name, He may give it you. John xv.4,5,16.

How could the disciples who were branches of the True Vine bring forth the fruit of the Spirit if the Holy Spirit had not been given? There is no difficulty about the answer if we rightly divide the Word of Truth, and recognise the essential difference between the Spirit of Christ and the Holy Spirit.

Fruit is the product of the Spirit of Christ:

And this I pray, that your love may abound yet more and more in knowledge and in all judgment; that ye may approve things that are excellent; that ye may be sincere and without offence till the day of Christ; being filled with the fruits of righteousness, which are by Jesus Christ, unto the glory and praise of God. Phil.i.9-11.

Gifts are bestowed by the Holy Spirit.

Now concerning spiritual gifts, brethren, I would not have you ignorant. Now there are diversities of gifts, but the same Spirit... But all these worketh that one and the self-same Spirit, dividing to every man severally as He will. 1Cor.xii.1,4-11.

Oft-times we have had to correct Bible students who

have failed to see the difference. The Holy Spirit, who divides the gifts amongst the members of the Body of Christ will not take up His abode in the believer who at the time does not manifest the fruit of the Spirit. In our own experience we have come across many people who, when they began to seek the baptism of the Spirit, had to make restitution and straighten up certain things of their past life. They were sanctified by the Spirit of God, and happenings that had sunk down in the subconscious self were resurrected, such as old quarrels, questionable dealings, uncharitable criticism, un-Christ-like attitude towards other Christians. These had to be dealt with one by one until all had been settled in scriptural fashion. Then, and not until then, did the Holy Spirit come in, filling and overflowing the human temple with rivers of living water. It is true that a believer might backslide after receiving the gift of the Holy Spirit, and even after receiving of His miraculous gifts, for the reception of the Holy Spirit does not mean that the recipients are immune from temptation and sin. Indeed it does seem as if baptised believers are tempted more after the Baptism than before. The great threefold temptation of our Lord in which the battle of life was fought, took place soon after the Holy Spirit had fallen upon Him.

Now when all the people were baptised, it came to pass, that Jesus also being baptised and praying, the heaven was opened, and the Holy Ghost descended in a bodily shape like a dove upon Him, and a voice came from heaven, which said, Thou art My beloved Son; in Thee I am well pleased. Luke iii.21,22.

And Jesus being full of the Holy Ghost returned from Jordan, and was led by the Spirit into the wilderness, being forty days tempted of the Devil... Luke iv.1,2.

The fruit of the Spirit is the outcome of the regenerated life, and is produced by the Spirit of Christ who dwells within the inheritors of the Kingdom of God. In the 5th chapter of Galatians we have the contrast shown between the works of the flesh, that are manifested in those who do not inherit the Kingdom, and the fruit of the Spirit in those who are in the Kingdom of God.

Works of the flesh: Non-inheritors of the Kingdom.
Now the works of the flesh are manifest, which are these; Adultery, fornication, uncleanness, lasciviousness, idolatry, witchcraft, hatred, variance, emulations, wrath, strife, seditions, heresies, envyings, murders, drunkenness, revel-lings, and such like: of the which I tell you before, as I have also told you in time past, that they which do such things shall not inherit the kingdom of God. Gal.v.19-21.

Fruit of the Spirit: Inheritors of the Kingdom.
But the fruit of the Spirit is love, joy, peace, longsuffering, gentleness, goodness, faith, meekness, temperance: against such there is no law, And they that are Christ's have crucified the flesh with the affections and lusts. If we live in the Spirit, let us also walk in the Spirit. Gal.v.22-25.

How often have we heard the ignorant remarks by some who oppose the baptism of the Holy Spirit: *"We are more anxious for the baptism of love than to have the baptism of tongues,"* or, *"It is more glorifying to God to seek the fruit than to seek the gifts."* These and many others of a similar kind reveal great ignorance on the part of the opponents. There is no such thing as a baptism of love to be found in the Bible. Love is not a baptism; it is the fruit of the Spirit of Christ which indwells every believer. It is true that speaking in tongues generally accompanies the outpouring of the Holy Spirit in our day, as it did in the New Testament, but there is no baptism of tongues. The attitude of some students of the Bible and other Christians towards the multitudinous and world-wide company of their fellow Christians, who have experienced the baptism of the Holy Spirit with miraculous signs, reveals a lack of love and sometimes insincerity. Let such remember that they might be called upon to straighten up such matters in their own lives when conviction reigns and the truth seizes upon them. It is difficult to see how honest men of God can oppose the truth which is so clear in the Bible, and so evident in their midst. In our own beloved British Isles the body that stands for this truth is far ahead of all others in the line of evangelism, and also in establishing churches in scriptural order. The great body of believers that is seeing souls saved on a colossal scale, holding the largest spiritual conventions of believers in the country, baptising thousands of converts yearly in water and celebrating the Lord's Supper in the largest gatherings of born-again people ever held in the whole world, and that is the means of changing and transforming the lives of thousands, is the body that stands for the baptism of the Holy Spirit and the restoration of the miraculous gifts.

The Nine Miraculous Gifts. The word of wisdom.

For to one is given by the Spirit the word of wisdom... 1Cor.xii.8.

Covet earnestly the best gifts is the inspired injunction to all believers, and the question has often been asked, *Which are the best gifts?* The correct answer is undoubtedly that wisdom and knowledge are pre-eminently among the best, for the simple reason that the other seven would be of little service to the Church without these two solid foundation gifts. We do not judge them to be the best because they stand at the head of the list of miraculous gifts in 1 Corinthians xii. To declare that they are best because they come first is to assume a strict standard for judging such matters that is not scriptural. Love, as compared with Faith and Hope, is explicitly said to be the best of the three, yet it is found at the bottom of the list. Without wisdom and knowledge we might have faith to remove mountains, to heal the sick, to work miracles, to prophesy, to discern spirits, to speak in tongues and to interpret, and yet bring the cause of Christ into absolute disrepute. We contend that the seven gifts should be guarded, guided, and controlled by the utterance of wisdom and the utterance of knowledge, if excrescences and extravagances are to be avoided in the Church. Note that it is called a *"word of wisdom,"* not a gift of wisdom. Herein lies a big difference, which should be observed by all who would rightly understand the significance of this gift of a word of wisdom. It is not natural wisdom which seems to be the heritage of some privileged people. It is a supernatural giving of a word of wisdom to believers by revelation, to the intent that they might advise, instruct, and speak the words of wisdom to the Church thereby making known the deep things of God. Paul evidently referred to this word of wisdom when he said, *"We speak, not in the words which man's wisdom teacheth, but which the Holy Ghost teacheth..."* (1Cor.ii.13). Then again, the gift of the word of wisdom is surely needed in times of testing and crisis. There are occasions when individuals as well as churches need the assistance of those who possess this supernatural gift. At times when important decisions, perplexing circumstances, and difficult problems have to be considered, we have often noticed the all-decisive word of wisdom fall from the lips of some faithful child of God in the time of need. There are instances of the use of this practical gift throughout the Scriptures.

Stephen.

And Stephen, full of faith and power, did great wonders and miracles among the people. Then there arose certain of the synagogue, which is called the synagogue of the Libertines, and Cyrenians, and Alexandrians, and of them of Cilicia and of Asia, disputing with Stephen.

And they were not able to resist the wisdom and the spirit by which he spake. Acts vi.8-10,

The word of knowledge.

...To another the word of knowledge by the same Spirit. 1Cor.xii.8.

It is not the knowledge that is acquired through mind-training at a seminary. It is not the natural ability to explain, to analyse, or to pursue to a logical conclusion. Neither is it a gift of knowledge, which like eternal life is given once and for all. It is the bestowal of a word of knowledge on special occasions. It ' 121 differs from the word of wisdom in that it miraculously supplies the mind with the knowledge of things. The former wisely decides after reviewing the matter under consideration, the latter reveals the matter itself. Spirit-filled preachers and teachers have again and again experienced the benefit of this gift, and they have often been amazed at their own utterances. So great has been the effect of the word of knowledge that at times it has seemed as if the mind had been enlarged. We have known anointed preachers who through the instrumentality of this gift speak on themes and subjects in their inspired discourses with which they themselves were little conversant, the Holy Spirit, through the gift of the word of knowledge, miraculously providing the material for their intellectual faculties. Under the anointing of the Spirit, the word of knowledge has been given, and passages of Scripture hitherto dark and obscure have been lit up and made clear through its Divine illumination.

It is obvious to all that a person might possess a store of knowledge with very little wisdom. He may also have little knowledge with a great deal of wisdom. We have known persons who have sadly lacked the word of wisdom when dispensing the word of knowledge entrusted to them.

We have also known others who have possessed comparatively little of the word of knowledge, who have displayed a great deal of the word of wisdom. It is most important that the ministry of the one should be balanced by the ministry of the other. There will be no danger of extravagances in the use of the other seven miraculous gifts, if they are safeguarded and controlled by wisdom and knowledge.

In Scripture there are several occasions recorded when knowledge of persons, places, and things has been miraculously communicated to the mind. A perfect example of the word of wisdom being coupled with the word of knowledge is found in the following Scripture. *Settle it therefore in your hearts, not to meditate before what ye shall answer: for I will give you a mouth and wisdom, which all your adversaries shall not be able to gainsay nor*

resist. Luke xxi.14,15.
"I will give you a mouth [the word of knowledge] *and wisdom* [the word of wisdom]*."*
Faith.
To another faith by the same Spirit. 1Cor.xii.9.
This is not the saving faith which a sinner exercises in Christ as Saviour when converted. It is a special giving of faith to those who are already members of the body of Christ. The Holy Spirit, in dividing His gifts among the children of God, bestows upon some of them special faith for special occasions. We have known faith given in this manner to have lifted servants of God entirely out of themselves, until they could believe for the impossible to happen. We have also known the same men, without this special enduement, to appear as helpless as children. At one time the preacher is ministering to the sick in the ordinary realms of faith with very little apparent result; at another he is moving amongst them, clothed with this special faith, and helpless cripples are healed to the astonishment of even the minister himself. Without this special faith he might feel weak and tired before the smallest of congregations, but with it he feels that monster congregations are in the palms of his hands. This special quality of faith
seems to come upon certain of God's servants at times of great need. Great occasions have sometimes called for more than ordinary faith and it is just then that it has been given. It is a gift that can be exercised with far-reaching results in the Kingdom, and the children of God should continually pray for its manifestation. Undoubtedly it was this special giving of faith that caused special miracles to be wrought through Paul at Ephesus. *And God wrought special miracles by the hands of Paul:*

so that from his body were brought unto the sick handkerchiefs or aprons, and the diseases departed from them, and the evil spirits went out of them. Acts xix.11,12.

Gifts of healing.

...*To another the gifts of healing by the same Spirit. 1Cor.xii.9.*

The root meaning of the word healing is "*a gradual recovery.*" Herein seems to lie the distinction between Divine healing and working of miracles. The former seems to imply that a person can through the exercise of this gift be gradually restored to health. The latter suggests an immediate Divine interposition, as a result of which a person is instantaneously healed. Both were in evidence during our Lord's ministry. To the leper Jesus said, "*I will; be thou clean*": and immediately the leprosy departed from him. To the nobleman Jesus said, "*Go thy way; thy son liveth,*" and the nobleman's son "*began to amend*" from that hour. It is a mistake to suppose that the person to whom the gifts of healing are given should immediately heal everybody. We have often been told by the unlearned that if we claim the power to heal we should visit the hospitals and sanatoria of our land, and heal all that are sick.

It cannot be denied that the Apostles possessed this gift to a remarkable degree, but we do not read that they did anything of the kind. Even in our Lord's ministry there were some who were not healed. We only read of one being healed out of the multitude at the pool of Bethesda. It is specifically stated that on one occasion He only healed a few sick folk in his own country, and marvelled at their unbelief. This wonderful gift, though given only to certain believers, does not preclude all believers from laying hands on the sick according to Mark xvi, or elders from anointing with oil according to James v.14. It is given in addition to these ordinary ministrations.

And these signs shall follow them that believe; In My name... they shall lay hands on the sick and they shall recover. Mark xvi.17,18.

Is any sick among you? let him call for the elders of the church; and let them pray over him, anointing him with oil in the name of the Lord; and the prayer of faith shall save the sick, and the Lord shall raise him up... James v.14,15.

Miracles.

To another the working of miracles... 1 Cor.xii.10.

"*The days of miracles are past!*" We could easily understand a statement of this kind coming from unbelievers, but certainly not from Christians. Such an attitude is not consistent with belief in the Christian religion. It would be just as easy to divorce Christianity from revelation to-day as to divorce it from the supernatural. If this particular gift of working of miracles is not for the Church to-day, the same applies to the other eight in the list, for we cannot distinguish between the gifts. A church without wisdom, knowledge, faith and discernment would indeed be a strange organism. Our Lord definitely transmitted the power to work miracles to His disciples. They went forth, and came back rejoicing because the demons were subject to them through His name. He again commissions them to preach the Gospel, and to expect miraculous signs after He was raised from the dead; and they went forth, God confirming their word with signs following. The early Church experienced the working of miracles, and these were used for the purpose of convincing people of the truth. The Acts of the Apostles is a record of continuous miracles from beginning to end. After the canon of Scripture was closed, history shows that miracles continued right down through the centuries to the present day.

Now ye are the body of Christ, and members in particular. And God hath set some in the church, first apostles, secondarily prophets, thirdly teachers, after that miracles, then gifts of healings, helps, governments, diversities of tongues. 1Cor.xii.27,28.

Prophecy.
...To another prophecy... 1Cor.xii.10.
The root meaning of the word is to foretell and to forthtell. This gift of inspired utterance is fully dealt with in *Chapter XII*.

Discerning of Spirits.
...To another discerning' of spirits... 1Cor.xii.10.
It does not follow that the person who has the gift of discernment can go about discerning everything and everybody. We have come across people of this kind and have been very glad to part company with them, for their gift of discernment has often turned out to be merely a gift of criticism. The person who exercises most discernment is often the person who makes the least claim to such a gift. It should not be confused with the natural intuition to detect certain tendencies and inclinations of men in the ordinary pursuits of life.

Some privileged folk have naturally a liberal supply of discernment in this respect, and as a consequence can avoid unprofitable associations with persons not congenial to them. But the gift of discernment has to do with the discerning of spirits of a supernatural order.

The Early Church had to contend with spiritual

powers that tried to hinder her in most subtle forms, and it was the right discernment that saved her from becoming involved through their intrigues. We are living at the close of the present dispensation, and if ever the Church was in the need of this spiritual gift it is to-day. The contention against spiritual wickedness in high places is greater than ever. The fight against principalities and powers is more fierce, and spiritual satanic forces leaving the loftier sphere are coming to earth as never before. Surely God is not allowing His children to become the prey of the enemy in these closing days of conflict!

He is restoring the miraculous gifts, including the gift of discerning of spirits, and His children are equipped to meet the enemy in the supernatural realm.

Divers kinds of tongues.

...To another divers kinds of tongues... 1Cor.xii.10.

The gift of speaking in tongues is dealt with in Chapter X.

Interpretation of tongues.

...To another the interpretation of tongues. 1Cor.xii.10.

The gift of interpretation is the companion gift to speaking in tongues, and both are distinctively reserved for the present dispensation. This gift is most essential to the profitable use of the gift of tongues, if the Church is to receive edification, for it translates from the spiritual into the intellectual. That is the reason why all who speak in tongues are exhorted to pray for interpretation. The Apostle gives clearly defined rules for the control of these gifts in the 14th chapter of his first epistle to the Corinthian Church. Evidently there was too much speaking in tongues in the assembly of the saints at Corinth, and too little interpretation. In regulating the use of the gifts he set a limit to the number of messages in tongues that should be given in one service, and insists upon the interpretation of each. If there is no interpreter the speaker who proposes to speak in tongues should be silent, speaking to himself and to God.

These clearly-defined rules show that the speaking in tongues can be controlled, and that the person in possession of the gift should know whether there is an interpreter present in the meeting. This brings us to the conclusion that there must be an acknowledged interpreter in the church, for this is the only means whereby the person present at the service can know. Nothing but disorder can ensue if persons are allowed to speak in tongues at will, without first of all knowing that an interpreter is present.

Then again, after years of experience in church life, we are persuaded that the exercise of the gifts, particularly tongues, interpretation, prophecy, and discernment, should be controlled and restricted to the members of the local church. Wise leaders of churches are always careful to see that unless a person is known or can produce credentials, he is not allowed to speak or minister. Why should they be less careful concerning strangers who move about from one place to another to exercise spiritual gifts?

Chapter 10. The Gift Of Tongues.

An unprecedented manifestation of the Spirit
And they were all filled with the Holy Ghost, and began to speak with other tongues, as the Spirit gave them utterance. Acts ii.4.

Amongst other signs and wonders which accompanied the great outpouring of the Holy Spirit at the commencement of the present dispensation, was the unprecedented marvel of speaking in tongues on the part of those who received. This phenomenon seems to be the distinctive sign of the new age, for it appears frequently throughout the Acts of the Apostles. The early Fathers have also testified to its continuance in the Church long after the days of the Apostles. We say *"distinctive sign"* because nothing like it had happened in the two previous Dispensations. Yet in those former days God gave many mighty manifestations of His Omnipotence, some of which we recall.

The Miraculous In The Dispensation Of The Father.
The Red Sea divided.
And Moses stretched out his hand over the sea; and the Lord caused the sea to go back by a strong east wind all that night, and made the sea dry land, and the waters were divided. And the children of Israel went into the midst of the sea upon the dry ground: and the waters were a wall unto them on their right hand, and on their left. Ex.xiv.21,22.

Water drawn from the rock.
Behold, I will stand before thee there upon the rock in Horeb; and thou shalt smite the rock, and there shall come water out

of it, that the people may drink. And Moses did so in the sight of the elders of Israel. Ex.xvii.6.

Wonders at Sinai.

And it came to pass on the third day in the morning, that there were thunders and lightnings, and a thick cloud upon the mount, and the voice of the trumpet exceeding loud; so that all the people that was in the camp trembled... And mount Sinai was altogether on a smoke, because the Lord descended upon it in fire: and the smoke thereof ascended as the smoke of a furnace, and the whole mount quaked greatly. Ex.xix.6-18.

The Glory in the Tabernacle.

Then a cloud covered the tent of the congregation, and the glory of the Lord filled the Tabernacle. Ex.xl.34.

Healing in the wilderness.

And the Lord said unto Moses, Make thee a fiery serpent, and set it upon a pole: and it shall come to pass, that every one that is bitten, when he looketh upon it, shall live. And Moses made a serpent of brass, and put it upon a pole, and it came to pass, that if a serpent had bitten any man, when he beheld the serpent of brass, he lived.
Num.xxi.8,9.

The walls of Jericho fall.

So the people shouted when the priests blew with the trumpets: and it came to pass, when the people heard the sound of the trumpet, and the people shouted with a great shout, that the wall fell down flat, so that the people went up into the city, every man straight before him, and they took the city. Joshua vi.20.

The servants of God in the Old Testament frequently experienced physical manifestations as they came under the power of God. We often wonder what some twentieth-century believers who object to the manifestation of the distinctive gift of tongues would say if they were called upon to witness some of the following incidents which are recorded in the Old Testament.

Samson's display of strength.

And when he came unto Lehi, the Philistines shouted against him: and the Spirit of the Lord came mightily upon him, and the cords that were upon his arms became as flax that was burnt with fire, and his bands loosed from off his hands. Judges xv.14.

And Samson called unto the Lord, and said, O Lord God, remember me, I pray thee, and strengthen me, I pray thee... And Samson took hold of the two middle pillars upon which the house stood... And he bowed himself with all his might; and the house fell upon the lords, and upon all the people that were therein... Judges xvi.28-30.

Daniel with his face to the ground.

Therefore I was left alone, and saw this great vision, and there remained no strength in me: for my comeliness was turned in me into corruption, and I retained no strength. Yet heard I the voice of His words: and when I heard the voice of His words, then was I in a deep sleep on my face, and my face toward the ground. And, behold, an hand touched me, which set me upon my knees, and upon the palms of my hands. Dan.x.8-10.

Ezekiel fell on his face.

...This was the appearance of the likeness of the glory of the Lord. And when I saw it, I fell upon my face... Ezek.i.28.

And the Spirit entered into me when He spake unto me, and set me upon my feet, that I heard Him that spake unto me. Ezek.li.2.

Tremblings and shakings.

Mine heart within me is broken because of the prophets;

all my bones shake; I am like a drunken man, and like a man whom the wine hath overcome, because of the Lord, and because of the words of His holiness. Jer.xxiii.9.

Quivering of the lips.
When I heard, my belly trembled; my lips quivered at the voice: rottenness entered into my bones, and I trembled in myself, that I might rest in the day of trouble... Hab.iii.16.

Preservation in fire.
And these three men, Shadrach, Meshach, and Abednego, fell down bound into the midst of the burning fiery furnace... And the princes, governors, and captains, and the king's counsellors, being gathered together, saw these men, upon whose bodies the fire had no power, nor was an hair of their head singed, neither were their coats changed, nor the smell of fire had passed on them. Dan.iii.23,27.

Visions.
Elisha's manservant.
And Elisha prayed, and said, Lord, I pray thee, open his eyes, that he may see. And the Lord opened the eyes of the young man; and he saw: and, behold, the mountain was full of horses and chariots of fire round about Elisha. 2Kings vi.17.

In the year that king Uzziah died I saw also the Lord sitting upon a throne, high and lifted up, and His train filled the temple. Isa.vi.1.

Ezekiel lifted by a lock of his head.
And it came to pass in the sixth year, in the sixth month, in the fifth day of the month, as I sat in mine house, and the elders of Judah sat before me, that the hand of the Lord God fell there upon me... And He put forth the form of an hand, and took me by the lock of mine head; and the Spirit lifted me up between the earth and the heaven, and brought me in the visions of God to Jerusalem... Ezek.viii.1,3.

The Old Testament abounds with proof that supernatural manifestations in the physical realm are no new phenomena. They have been frequently in evidence when men have been endued with power from God. History records such in the great revivals of the past, and why some people of to-day should be so incredulous regarding this particular aspect of the Spirit's operations it is difficult to understand. How often have we heard ministers and evangelists, when preaching on the need of revival, say, *"Oh for the good old days when the Spirit of God used to fall."* Yet these same men have deliberately rejected the present outpouring of the Holy Spirit because of its physical manifestations. We have known earnest Christians to spend whole nights in prayer for revival, yet when God answered in an outpouring of the Spirit which caused the least physical effect, they have resisted and even grieved the Spirit by their attitude. In the light of Bible revivals one begins to wonder if they are praying intelligently when they do not expect a movement in the physical as well as in the spiritual realm.

Let us glance at some of the supernatural manifestations during our Lord's earthly ministry.

The Miraculous In The Dispensation Of The Son. Nicodemus views the miraculous.

The same came to Jesus by night, and said unto him, Rabbi, we know that Thou art a Teacher come from God: for no man can do these miracles that Thou doest, except God be with him. John iii.2.

Evidence of Messiahship.

Now when John had heard in the prison the works of

Christ, he sent two of his disciples, and said unto Him, Art thou He that should come, or do we look for another? Jesus answered and said unto them, Go and shew John again those things which ye do hear and see: The blind receive their sight, and the lame walk, the lepers are cleansed, and the deaf hear, the dead are raised up, and the poor have the gospel preached to them. Matt.xi.2-5. **Miracles of all kinds abounded in the days of our Lord.**

Water was turned into wine; blind eyes were opened; deaf ears were unstopped; the tongue of the dumb was loosened; the lame walked; the paralysed limb was healed; vast multitudes were miraculously fed; the sea became a solid highway; a fish the custodian of tribute money; lepers were cleansed; the dead were raised; miraculous draughts of fishes were caught; the demon-possessed were delivered; the wind and waves rendered implicit obedience,—yet we do not read of anyone speaking in unknown tongues.

Distinctive Miracle In The Dispensation Of The Holy Ghost.

We shall now consider this distinctive miracle of utterance in languages, as it was experienced by various groups and also by individuals in the early Church.

At Jerusalem.

And when the day of Pentecost was fully come, they were all with one accord in one place. And suddenly there came a sound from heaven as of a rushing mighty wind, and it filled all the house where they were sitting. And there appeared unto them cloven tongues like as of fire, and it sat upon each of them. And they were all filled with the Holy Ghost, and began to speak with other tongues, as the Spirit gave them utterance. Acts ii.1-4.

At Jerusalem on the day of Pentecost the indwelling

power made the disciples reel like drunken men, and the multitudes could only account for such strange scenes upon the supposition that they were drunk with wine. Their actions were exactly like those who had come under the intoxicating influence of strong drink. Peter, without attempting to deny that the manifestations were strange, had to explain that this was the result of an outpouring of the Spirit according to an Old Testament prophecy. Paul in later years, when writing to the Church at Ephesus, must have known something of these experiences. The members of that church, too, must have been accustomed to spiritual intoxication, for the Apostle exhorts, *"Be not drunk with wine, wherein is excess; but be filled with the Spirit; speaking to yourselves in psalms and hymns and spiritual songs, singing and making melody in your heart to the Lord."* The extent to which a person can be intoxicated in the one realm was the same as in the other.

At Caesarea.

While Peter yet spake these words, the Holy Ghost fell on all them which heard the Word. And they of the circumcision which believed were astonished, as many as came with Peter, because that on the Gentiles also was poured out the gift of the Holy Ghost. For they heard them speak with tongues, and magnify God. Then answered Peter, Can any man forbid water, that these should not be baptised, which have received the Holy Ghost as well as we? Acts x.44-47.

At Caesarea some eight years later the Holy Spirit came on the Gentiles who were assembled in the house of Cornelius the centurion. On this occasion the Spirit came as Peter was preaching, and again the miraculous utterance of speaking in tongues was in evidence. This was the unquestioned manifestation that compelled them of the circumcision to see that the outpouring of the Spirit that day was the same as that received eight years earlier at Jerusalem. The miraculous languages were tangible manifestations beyond question or dispute, whereby an all-wise God had set His seal upon the Gentiles in a sovereign act that could not be withstood.

Undoubtedly this was the ground upon which Peter justified himself later for going unto them. The serious charge brought against him of opening the door to the Gentiles was silenced by the declaration: *"As I began to speak, the Holy Ghost fell on them, as on us at the beginning. Forasmuch then as God gave them the like gift as He did unto us, who believed on the Lord Jesus Christ, what was I, that I could withstand God?"*

The traditional prejudices and age-long beliefs of an entire race were swept away before the incoming power. There was no doubt in the mind of anyone, for they heard them speak with tongues and magnify God. The impregnable wall of partition that had stood between nations for centuries like the walls of Jericho fell at the sound of those wonderful tongues.

At Ephesus.
When they heard this, they were baptised in the name of the Lord Jesus. And when Paul had laid his hands upon them, the Holy Ghost came on them, and they spake with tongues, and prophesied. Acts xix.5,6.

At Ephesus the outpouring of the Spirit was accompanied by speaking in tongues and prophecy. The latter gift was not given to the disciples at Pentecost, neither is it mentioned in connection with the outpouring at Caesarea. The speaking in tongues was certainly a most frequent sign of the baptism of the Holy

Spirit in the days of the Apostles. Why some Christian teachers should object to this sign in our day is difficult to understand, more especially when we are living in the latter end of the very Dispensation that is destined to witness a greater outpouring than at the beginning. The one great difficulty to our mind is the reading into the Acts of the Apostles changes of dispensations that do not exist. We have come across so many of these dispensational experts that there is scarcely a promise of supernatural power in the Bible that is not ruled out for the poor believer of the twentieth century. To-day there are scores if not hundreds of books and pamphlets written by opposers to show that the miraculous gifts are not for these days, yet tens of thousands of the most saintly people all over the world are actually experiencing them.

**References To Tongues
In The Epistles.
The First Corinthian
Epistle.**

For if I pray in an unknown tongue, my spirit prayeth, but my understanding is unfruitful. 1Cor.xiv.14. Note.— Praying with the Spirit means praying in an unknown tongue (his understanding is unfruitful). Whereas praying with the understanding means praying in his own tongue (his understanding is fruitful).

I will sing with the Spirit, and I will sing with the understanding also. 1Cor.xiv.15.

Note.—Singing with the Spirit means singing in an unknown tongue (his understanding is unfruitful). Whereas singing with the understanding means singing in his own tongue (his understanding is fruitful).

If praying with the Spirit in verse 14 means praying in an unknown tongue, then singing with the Spirit in verse 15 must certainly mean singing in an unknown tongue.

The inspired Apostle here testifies to the blessed experience of praying and singing in heavenly languages. In the silence of his own room, when in private devotion, he effectively poured out the fullness of his heart in words uttered by the Spirit. Those spiritual songs given to him in words, not intelligible to his understanding, and with tunes not composed by the human mind, were supernatural means of communion and edification that enraptured his soul.

The Ephesian Epistle.

And be not drunk with wine, wherein is excess; but be filled with the Spirit; speaking to yourselves in psalms and hymns and spiritual songs, singing and making melody in your heart to the Lord. Eph.v.18,19.

We know that hymns are *"songs of praise"* and psalms are *"sacred songs,"* but what are the spiritual songs that are linked up with them? Surely the Apostle did not mean psalms and hymns and spiritual psalms, or psalms and hymns and spiritual hymns, for this would mean unnecessary and causeless repetition. This same Apostle in his first letter to the Corinthians has been most careful to explain the difference between singing with the understanding and singing with the Spirit. He testifies to the fact that when he sang with the understanding his understanding was fruitful, but when he sang with the Spirit his understanding was unfruitful. With his understanding he could sing psalms and hymns that were intelligible to his mind, but when he sang with the Spirit, the words were unintelligible, for he was singing in unknown tongues— making melody in his heart to God in spiritual songs. In this connection the exhortation given to the Ephesians is most significant. They were not to be drunk with wine, wherein is excess, but they were to be filled with the Spirit. The disciples who spoke in tongues on the day of Pentecost were filled with the Spirit, and they were like drunken men. The Apostle is here exhorting these Ephesian believers to go in for the same spiritual intoxication. The comparison is between those who are drunk with wine, and those who are drunk with the Spirit. The extent in the one realm is as wide as its extent in the other.

The Colossian Epistle.

Let the word of Christ dwell in you richly in all wisdom; teaching and admonishing one another in psalms and hymns and spiritual songs, singing with grace in your hearts to the Lord. Col.iii.16.

Here again spiritual songs are singled out from psalms and hymns just as they were in the Ephesian Epistle. The songs in which the understanding is fruitful are mentioned before those in which the understanding is unfruitful. To all who have experienced singing with the Spirit the order is most natural. We have known many cases of individual believers, and also whole assemblies, large and small, to have started praising God in psalms and hymns, when suddenly the Spirit has taken possession of their vocal organs, and they have been switched off into heavenly anthems in unknown tongues, with tunes given by the Spirit. They seemed to have reached a plane in worship where their mother tongue was far too inadequate to express the deep longings of the soul. During those soul-enrapturing experiences, the understanding has been unfruitful, as Paul

explains, but God has been magnified and the soul edified. We have often proved that the soul can reach spiritual altitudes in worship where all earthly languages are expressionless. Psalms and hymns have carried the soul out in praise; in our own experience the richer and fuller Welsh language has sent it heavenward; but we have sometimes reached an altitude where spiritual songs are the only means of expressing our love and adoration to God. **Prophecy in the Thessalonian Epistle.**
Quench not the Spirit. Despise not prophesyings. 1Thess.v.19, 20.
Those who declare that the miraculous gifts are not referred to in any of the Church Epistles except the first Corinthian Epistle must have read over the New Testament carelessly in this connection. Here again in the first Thessalonian Epistle we have a definite reference to one of the nine gifts of the Spirit. The injunction, Despise not prophesyings, would be meaningless unless the gift of prophecy was exercised in the Church. Like the mention of the gift of tongues in the Corinthian Epistle which needed regulating, the gift of prophecy is mentioned in this epistle because there was an evident disposition on the part of some to despise the prophetic utterance. The one big thing some Bible teachers seem to lose sight of is that the Church Epistles were written to churches whose normal experience was that of the supernatural in evidence. There would be no need for the mention of tongues even in Corinth if things were going along smoothly, and the gifts properly exercised. It seems as if the only occasions when they are referred to in the Epistles are when they call for instruction and correction. The idea of the gifts being withdrawn simply because they are not calling

for a prominent place in the Epistles is therefore absurd. Such a method of explaining scripture can only lead to confusion. We have seen that the miraculous gifts are referred to in at least four Church epistles.
Are Tongues Divine Or Satanic?
The power that takes possession of the vocal organs, and speaks and sings through a person in languages he has never learned, must certainly be supernatural. We have known choice saints who at the coming in of the Spirit have spoken in this way for hours, and in some instances for days, without being able to speak in their mother tongue. Thus the supernatural element of the experience makes it imperative that those in quest of truth should decide whether it is of God or Satan, for there are only two sources from which the power can emanate. We are not unmindful of psychic or emotional manifestations, but such are not at this juncture coming under our consideration. We are dealing with that which is absolutely supernatural. Therefore that which tens of thousands of believers in our day experience must either be of Divine or satanic origin.

It is impossible for any reasonable mind to come to any other logical conclusion. The Scriptures, our only sure guide in life, most certainly supply the acid test that can decide the question for the unprejudiced. The vast multitudes of believers all over the world who speak in tongues can be tested by their fruits. If they bear the fruit of the Spirit of Christ then they cannot be demon- possessed; if they do not bear the fruit of the Spirit of Christ then they cannot be Christ- possessed

Doth a fountain send forth at the same place sweet water and bitter? Can the fig tree, my brethren, bear olive berries? either a vine, figs? so can no fountain both yield

salt water and fresh. James iii.11,12.

But when the Pharisees heard it, they said, This fellow doth not cast out devils, but by Beelzebub the prince of the devils. And Jesus knew their thoughts, and said unto them, Every kingdom divided against itself is brought to desolation; and every city or house divided against itself shall not stand: And if Satan cast out Satan, he is divided against himself; how shall then his kingdom stand? ...Or else how can one enter into a strong man's house, and spoil his goods, except he first bind the strong man? and then he will spoil his house... A good man out of the good treasure of the heart bringeth forth good things: and an evil man out of the evil treasure bringeth forth evil things.—Matt.xii.24-35.

Vital Tests.

The house referred to in verse 29 is the whole being—body, soul and spirit, and it is impossible for it to be occupied by God and Satan at the same time. The supernatural speaking in tongues must therefore emanate from God or from Satan. Let us now apply the fruitage test to the great company of present-day believers who speak in tongues as the Spirit gives utterance:—

- They testify to the experience of regeneration.
- They stand for the whole Bible as the Word of God.
- They walk in holiness of life according to the Scriptures.
- They are most keen for the salvation of souls.
- They are obedient to the commandments of the

Lord.
- They preach and practice believer's baptism by immersion.
- They remember the Lord's death each first day of the week as the disciples did.
- They build on the impregnable rock of Fundamentalism.
- They insist on the fruit of the Spirit balancing the gifts of the Spirit.

This is the type of Christian who speaks in tongues in every country under the canopy of Heaven in our day. Surely it is not difficult to identify the fruit of the Spirit of Christ in such believers. There are occasional exceptions to the rule in general, as there are among all other Christian communities, but it is inconsiderate and uncharitable to condemn whole movements on account of isolated failures. The only possible conclusion to which any reasonable mind can come is that opposers of this supernatural movement are wrong and sadly mistaken in their views.

Chapter 11. The Utility Of Speaking In Tongues.

But the manifestation of the Spirit is given to every man to profit withal. 1Cor.xii.7.
Of the nine miraculous gifts of the Spirit the speaking in tongues arouses the greatest measure of opposition, from some who have been considered teachers in the Christian Church for years. There are obvious reasons why this particular gift should be so challenged on their part. The great outpouring of the Spirit with the miracle of speaking in tongues is taking place all over the world. Tens of thousands are rejoicing in the heaven-sent gift, and their numbers are increasing day by day. Then again this Latter Rain is not falling within the confines of any recognised religious body, its showers are being poured forth upon those who are called to bear the reproach of Christ outside the camp. These outstanding facts are not comforting, especially to those who have hastily put their opposition into print; hence the repudiation at all costs of this frequent gift of speaking in tongues which accompanies the present outpouring. The chief method of attack is to say that dear children of God are being side-tracked by the enemy, and the proof that this contention is correct is that they speak in tongues. Poor deluded teachers!

What a pity they do not humble themselves, and examine the Word of God afresh in the light of what is taking place around them. The following are six distinct uses in the New Testament for the speaking in tongues:—
To Confirm The Ministry Of Believers.
And these signs shall follow them that believe; In My

Name shall they cast out devils; they shall speak with new tongues... And they went forth, and preached everywhere, the Lord working with them, and confirming the Word with signs following. Amen. Mark xvi.17,20.

In Exceptional Cases To Convince Foreigners.

And they were all filled, with the Holy Ghost, and began to speak with other tongues, as the Spirit gave them utterance. And there were dwelling at Jerusalem Jews, devout men, out of every nation under heaven. Now when this was noised abroad, the multitude came together, and were confounded, because that every man heard them speak in his own language. Acts ii.4-6.

To Magnify God.

And they of the circumcision which believed were astonished, as many as came with Peter, because that on the Gentiles also was poured out the gift of the Holy Ghost. For they heard them speak with tongues, and magnify God. Acts x.45,46.

To Edify The Believer.

For he that speaketh in an unknown tongue speaketh not unto men, but unto God: for no man understandeth him; howbeit in the Spirit he speaketh mysteries... He that speaketh in an unknown tongue edifieth himself; but he that prophesieth edifieth the church. 1Cor.xiv.2,4.

To Edify The Church.

I would that ye all spake with tongues, but rather that ye prophesied; for greater is he that prophesieth than he that speaketh with tongues, except he interpret, that the church may receive edifying. 1Cor.xiv.5.

A Sign To Unbelievers.

Wherefore tongues are for a sign, not to them that believe, but to them that believe not... 1Cor.xiv.22.

The disciples at Pentecost had been speaking in

tongues, as the Spirit gave utterance, sometime before the multitudes gathered together. It was when "*it was noised abroad*" that the people came together, and understood what was spoken in tongues by the disciples. The gift of tongues, as we have already shown, is in some cases understood by foreigners. We shall now state a few cases to show that persons have had this experience in the great outpouring of the Spirit that is taking place in these last days. T. J. McCrossan, B.A., B.D., formerly teacher of Greek in Manitoba University, in his *Speaking with other Tongues: Sign or Gift?* testifies to the following: "The writer, like scores of other theological students, was taught that the Holy Spirit never took possession of people's tongues to-day, and made them praise God in another language. This only happened in Apostolic times, our professors told us. However, we now know that these honoured teachers were mistaken.

**Instances
In Evidence.
Praising God
in Chinese.**

"One night, after a great evangelistic meeting where scores had been saved, we saw the evangelist himself overcome by the power of God while in prayer, and we heard him speak Chinese. We recognized the language because we had so often heard it spoken; but God, in His goodness, had a Christian Alliance missionary standing by our side, a man we knew, trusted and loved. He had been a Chinese missionary for over eighteen years. He whispered to us, '*He is praising God in the very Chinese dialect I preach in; he is speaking it perfectly, and oh, how he is praising the Lord Jesus.*' He then interpreted sentence after sentence to us. It was indeed wonderful, as we both knew that the evangelist was absolutely ignorant of the Chinese language."

Praising the Lord in Norwegian.

"On another occasion we heard an American woman, when filled with the Holy Ghost, praise God in Norwegian. We knew it was either Norwegian or Swedish, for we had heard these languages so frequently in Minneapolis. However, our gracious Lord had a Norwegian gentleman standing by our side, who said, *'Brother McCrossan, I know this woman. She is an American and utterly ignorant of my language (Norwegian), and yet she is speaking it perfectly, and oh, sir, I have never heard anyone praise the Lord Jesus as she is doing.'*"

Praising the Lord in French.

"On another occasion we heard a person praising the Lord Jesus in perfect French, one who was utterly ignorant of that language.

"We have frequently heard young people both speak and sing in other tongues, as the Spirit gave them utterance; singing with a voice so vastly superior to their own natural voice, that there was no comparison. No interpreter was present on these occasions, and yet we felt certain these were genuine languages (having studied five different languages), and we knew from the tone, the facial expression, and the marvellous joy, that it was the work of the Holy Spirit. There was something about it so sweet, so attractive, so helpful; something that actually drew one into the very presence of God."

The following is culled from a remarkable book, *With Signs Following*, by our esteemed brother, Stanley H. Frodsham:

Marathi woman speaks in English.

"A gracious Pentecostal revival came to Mukti, the home where Pandita Ramabai had gathered some two thousand widows and orphans under her care. In the early part of 1907, Albert Norton, that venerable missionary of Dhond, wrote: 'About six months ago we began to hear of Christian believers in different places and countries receiving the gift of speaking in a new tongue, which they had never known before. Our hearts were stirred by these accounts, some of them having come from those whom we have known for years as most humble, earnest, and devoted servants of the Lord. One week ago to-day, I visited the Mukti mission at Kedgaon, thirteen miles from here.

"Miss Abrams asked me if I would not like to go into a room where about twenty girls were praying. After entering, I knelt by a table on one side, with closed eyes. Presently I heard someone near me praying very distinctly in English... I was struck with astonishment, as I knew that there was no one in the room who could speak English, besides Miss Abrams. I opened my eyes, and within three feet of me, on her knees, with closed eyes and raised hands, was a woman, whom I had baptised at Kedgaon in 1899, nearly eight years ago, and whom my wife and I had known intimately since as a devoted Christian worker. Her mother-tongue was Marathi, and she could speak a little Hindustani. But she was utterly unable to speak or understand English, such as she was using. But when I heard her speak English idiomatically, distinctly, and fluently, I was impressed as I would have been had I seen one, whom I knew to be dead, raised to life. A few other illiterate Marathi women and girls were speaking in English, and some were speaking in other languages which none of us at Kedgaon understood.

This was not gibberish, but it closely resembled the speaking of foreign languages to which I have listened but did not understand. "Again, I was at Mukti last Saturday and Lord's Day, where some twenty-four persons had received the gift of tongues. Quite a number had received the ability to speak in English, a language before unknown to them. Just why God enabled these women and girls to speak in English, instead of Tamil, Bengali, Tugulu, or some other language of India, unknown to them, I cannot say. But I have an idea that it is in mercy to us poor missionaries from Europe and America, who, as a class, seem to be doubting Thomases in regard to the gifts and workings of the Spirit, and are not receiving the power of the Holy Ghost as we ought, and we shall wish that we had done, when we are entered into the world to come."

Tongues used to convert Jewish doctor.
"Another instance of a Hebrew being saved through the ministry of speaking in tongues is that of Dr. Florence Murcutt, now of Manhattan Beach, California, who is an Australian Jewess and was brought up in the Jewish faith. She was taught by her mother that she must never believe that Jesus was the Son of God. Having an enquiring mind, on the death of her mother, she read through the whole Word of God from cover to cover in six weeks. After having secured her medical degree in the city of Philadelphia, she first came in contact with the Pentecostal people in Vancouver, British Columbia... She was travelling down from Vancouver to Los Angeles, and stopped off at Portland, Oregon, where there was a Pentecostal camp meeting. She saw the signs following, and there were many saved and healed and filled with the Spirit in this meeting. One night she

stood close by the tent where there were ten Canadians standing. She was conversing with them when one Canadian brother, who was under the anointing of God, began to speak to her, addressing her in the purest Parisian French, a language with which she was familiar. Dr. Murcutt says: '*He told me I was a sinner, and that I could only be saved in one way, and that was through Jesus Christ who was the Way, the Truth, and the Life. He told me that Jesus was the Door, and that I would have to enter by that door. He told me that He was the Bread of Life, and that I would have to be sustained by Him. As he spoke he urged me to yield to God. This brother was absolutely unfamiliar with Parisian French, but was speaking entirely under the anointing of God. He told me that this Pentecostal outpouring was of God, and that it was the Latter Rain which God had promised to send in the last days. The Spirit through him gave a full revelation of the truth concerning the Trinity... We talked for over an hour in Parisian French. When I said anything that tallied with the Word of God, the Spirit of God in this brother rejoiced. When I said anything contrary to the Word of God, the Spirit of God in him would moan. As a result of this manifestation of God's presence, I went on my knees and yielded to God.*' For many years Dr. Murcutt has been serving the Lord, and has been greatly blessed as an evangelist among both English-speaking people and Latin Americans."

Africans in Congo speak English.

"That first wonderful meeting lasted from ten a.m. till three p.m. For three hours the whole place was swayed by God's Spirit. Many fell as though dead, and those who had no room to fall on the floor, fell upon each other. At least two cases occurred of those who praised God in beautiful English, and I also heard snatches of French and Dutch, or German. And almost all who spoke in tongues had languages with beautifully clear 'R' sounds, which is significant since in the natural a Luban cannot pronounce this sound..."

Minister suddenly speaks in native language.
"A company of Indians from Fisher River and other Indian reservations, about two hundred miles north of Winnipeg, hearing of this gracious outpouring, came to see for themselves. Soon they were down on their faces before God, and a number of them received this wonderful Baptism. On the return of these Indians to their reservations a remarkable revival broke out in their midst, and God's Word truly was confirmed with signs and wonders, and divers miracles and gifts of the Holy Ghost.

"One of the first to receive the Baptism in those early days was Pastor A. G. Ward, who went out to preach among the Indians of the Fisher River reservation. He had to speak through an interpreter. One day when he was preaching under the power of the Spirit, he began to speak in other tongues and his interpreter suddenly exclaimed, *'Why, you are now speaking to us in our own language.'* It was a call for these Indians to advance, and this remarkable manifestation had a marked effect on the hearers."

We believe that thousands of such testimonies could be tabulated if time and space would permit, but the above will suffice to convince any reasonable and unprejudiced person that God is doing to-day what He did at Pentecost.

We are now drawing your attention to a remarkable scene where the glossolalia was in evidence among the early Christians at Rome.

A Pentecostal Meeting In The Days Of Nero.
Historical Description from the Writings Of The Late Dean Farrar.

Amongst the many writers on the first days of Christianity the late Dean Farrar stands out as a learned and recognised historical authority. In his *Darkness to Dawn*, illustrating the dawn of Christianity upon the darkness of Paganism, he states, *"Those who are familiar with the literature of the first century will recognise that even for the minutest allusions and particulars I have contemporary authority."* The Dean describes a secret visit of the young Roman prince Britannicus, brother of Nero, whose heart was strongly drawn to the faith, to a meeting held by the early Christians in a granary. To the tens of thousands in the present day who are acquainted with the distinctive features of worship in a meeting where the Spirit is poured forth, the historical description will be most interesting.

"The room in which the Christians met was a large granary in which Plautius stored the corn which came from his Sicilian estates. It was as well lighted as circumstances admitted, but chiefly by the torches and lanterns of those who had come from all parts of the city to be present at this winter evening assembly. "Britannicus was astonished at their numbers. He was quite unaware that a religion so strange— a religion of yesterday, whose founder had perished in Palestine little more than twenty years before—already numbered such a multitude of adherents in the Imperial city. Clemens whispered to him that this was but one congregation, and represented only a fraction of the entire number of believers in Rome, who formed a multitude which no single room could have accommodated... If Britannicus was surprised by the numbers of the Christians, he was still more surprised by their countenances. The majority were slaves, whose native home was Greece or Asia. Their faces bore the stamp which had been fixed on them by years of toil and hardship; but even on the worn features of the aged there was something of the splendour and surprise of the Divine secret. The young prince saw that they were in possession of something more divine than the world could understand. For the first time he beheld not one or two only, but a blessed company of faithful people who had felt the peace of God which passeth all understanding.

"The children also filled him with admiration. He had seen lovely slaves in multitudes; there were throngs of them in the Palace, and in the houses of men like Otho and Petronius. But their beauty was the beauty of the flesh alone. How little did it resemble the sweet and sacred innocence which brightened the eyes of these boys and girls who had been brought up in the shelter of Christian homes!

"But he was struck most of all with the youths. How many Roman youths had he seen who had been trained in wealthy households, in whom had been fostered from childhood every evil impulse of pride and passion! ...Many of them had inherited the haughty beauty of patrician generations; but luxury and wine had left their marks upon them, and if they had been set side by side with these, whose features glowed with health and purity and self-control, how would the pallid faces of those dandies have looked...

"Nothing could have been more simple than the order of worship... They had no distinctive dress, but wore the ordinary tunic or cloak of daily life, though evidently the best and neatest that they could procure. In such a community, so poor, so despised, there could be no pomp of ritual, but the lack of it was more than compensated by the reverent demeanour which made each Christian feel that, for the time being, this poor granary was the house of God and the gate of heaven. They knelt or stood in prayer, as though the mud floor were sacred as the rocks of Sinai, and every look and gesture was happy, as of those who felt that not only angels and archangels were among them, but the invisible presence of their Lord Himself.

"First they prayed; and Britannicus had never before heard real prayers. But here were men and women, the young and the old, to whom prayer evidently meant direct communion with the Infinite and the Unseen; to whom the solitude of private supplication, and the community of worship, were alike admissions into the audience-chamber of the Divine...

"But a new and yet more powerful sensation was kindled in his mind, when at the close of the prayers they sang a hymn... Britannicus listened entranced to the mingled voices as they rose and fell in exquisite cadence. He had heard in theatres all the most famous singers of Rome; he had heard the chosen youths and maidens chanting in the temple processions; he had heard the wailing over the dead, and the Thalassio chorus of the bridal song. But he had heard nothing which distantly resembled this melody and harmony of voices wedded to holy thoughts; and, although there were no instruments, the angelical, soft, trembling voices, seemed to him like echoes from some new and purer region of existence... When the hymn was over they sat down, and Linus rose to speak to them a few words of exhortation. He reminded them that they had been called from darkness to light, and from the power of Satan unto God. He told them that they had fled to the rock of Christ amid a weltering sea of human wickedness, and though the darkness was around them he bade them to walk in the light, since they were the children of light...

"Were not their bodies temples of the Holy Ghost which dwelt in them, except they were reprobates? ... The world was passing away and the fashion of it; their own lives were but as the withering grass and the fading flower; and was not the day of the Lord at hand? ...

"So far had he proceeded when a mighty answering '*Maranatha*' of the deeply-moved assembly smote the air, and immediately afterwards Britannicus stood transfixed and thrilled to the very depths of his whole being.

"For now a voice such as he had never heard—a sound unearthly and unaccountable— seemed not only to strike his ears, but to grasp his very heart. It was awful in its range, its tone, its modulations, its startling, penetrating, appalling power; and although he was unable to understand its utterance, it seemed to convey the loftiest eloquence of religious transport, thrilling with rapture and conviction. And, in a moment or two, other voices joined in. The words they spoke were exalted, intense, impassioned, full of mystic significance. They did not speak in their ordinary familiar tongue, but in what seemed to be as it were the essence and idea of all languages, though none could tell whether it was Hebrew, or Greek, or Latin, or Persian. It resembled now one and now the other, as some overpowering and unconscious impulse of the moment might direct. The burden of the thoughts of the speakers seemed to be the ejaculation of ecstasy, of amazement, of thanksgiving, of supplication, of passionate dithyramb or psalm. They spoke not to each other, or to the congregation, but seemed to be addressing their inspired soliloquy to God. And among these strange sounds of many voices, all raised in sweet accord of entranced devotion, there were some which no one could rightly interpret. The other voices seemed to interpret themselves. They needed no translation into significant language, but spontaneously awoke in the hearts of the hearers the echo of the impulse from which they sprang. There were others which rang on the air more sharply, more tumultuously, like the clang of a cymbal or the booming of hollow brass, and they conveyed no meaning to any but the speakers, who in producing these barbarous tones, felt carried out of themselves.

But there was no disorderly tumult in various voices. They were reverberations of one and the same supernatural ecstasy—echoes awakened in different consciousnesses by one and the same intense emotion.

"Britannicus had heard the *glossolalia*—the gift of the tongue. He had been a witness of the Pentecostal marvel, a phenomenon which heathendom had never known.

"Nor had he only heard it, or witnessed it. For as the voices began to grow fainter, as the whole assembly sat listening in the hush of awful expectation, the young prince himself felt as if a spirit passed before him, and the hair of his flesh stood up; he felt as if a Power and a Presence stronger than his own dominated his being; annihilated his inmost self; dealt with him as a player does who sweeps the strings of an instrument into concord or discord at his will. He felt ashamed of the impulse; he felt terrified by it; but it breathed all over and around and through him, like the mighty wind; it filled his soul as with ethereal fire; it seemed to inspire, to uplift, to dilate his very soul; and finally it swept him onward as with numberless rushings of congregated wings. The passion within him was burning into irresistible utterance, and, in another moment, through that humble throng of Christians would have rung in impassioned music the young voice of the last of the Claudii pouring forth things unutterable, had not the struggle ended by his uttering one cry, and then sinking into a faint. Before that unwonted cry from the voice of a boy the assembly sank into silence, and after two or three moments the impulse left him.

Panting, unconscious, not knowing where he was, or whether he had spoken or not, or how to explain or account for the heart-shaking inspiration which had seemed to carry him out of himself beyond all mountain barriers and over unfathomable seas... Meanwhile, as the hour was late, and they all had to get home in safety through the dark streets and lanes through which they had come—some of them from considerable distances—Linus rose, and with uplifted hand dismissed the congregation.

"'*The escort is waiting,*' said Pudens.

"So they bade farewell to Pomponia, and the soldiers saw them safely to the Palace.

"When they had started, Claudia said: '*Oh, Pomponia, while he was at the gathering the Power came upon him; he seemed scarcely able to resist it; but for his fainting I believe that he would have spoken with the tongue!*'" Dean Farrar in this description of the meeting among the early Christians at Rome has given in the main an accurate account of the happenings at a present-day meeting where the same Holy Spirit is poured forth. Striking beyond all else we have read is the similarity of the scene in the granary with many we have ourselves witnessed. In the first place the despised slaves which comprised the congregation, like the followers of Pentecost to-day, could not boast in any wealth of splendour or ritual. Then again the place of worship was a barn for storing corn, and this reminds us that although nineteen hundred years have passed, God is still pouring out His Spirit in unusual places. The first company of our own Elim workers came under the outpouring of the Holy Spirit in a barn in Monaghan at the commencement of our work. The unrestrained outpourings of the heart similar to what occurred in the granary are taking place to-day in thousands of Pentecostal assembles all over the world. Singing in the Spirit with a supernatural melody, like that which the slaves of Rome experienced in their worship, is being experienced in Pentecostal churches everywhere today. Truly the Dean has delineated from age-long history the true Scriptural phenomena of the outpouring of the Holy Spirit in this the twentieth century.

Chapter 12. The Gift Of Prophecy.

...To another prophecy. 1Cor.xii.10.
We are not at this juncture entering into the possible distinction between the office of the prophet and the gift of prophecy. The gift was evidently most common in the early Church, whereas the office was limited to a clearly-defined class who were designated *"prophets."* Our purpose is to deal with the subject in its broadest aspect, which covers the whole field of inspired utterance. The definition of the terms *"forth-telling'* ' and *"foretelling"'* will give us the right perspective in our survey of the subject, and will enable us to differentiate between these aspects in the use of the gift in the early Church. At the outset we should bear in mind that the only true pattern of the Church is drawn clearly with unerring hand upon the pages of the New Testament. Any attempt to introduce practices or systems that deviate from the pattern can only result in confusion in the Church, and bringing dishonour upon the Name of Christ. Then again it should be remembered that the protection of God against the powers of darkness cannot be claimed even by the child of God if he persists in adding to or taking away from that pattern.

Concerning the gift of prophecy, we are not approaching the subject as those who are inexperienced, for our wide range of Church work has brought us into very close contact with the varied aspects of the prophetic utterance, and we have always judged the matter in the light of the unfailing pattern. The gift of prophecy, when rightly guarded and controlled by the infallible written Word, is a means of high and true spiritual elevation for individual and church. But when used according to the dictates of the human mind without regard to the Scriptures, it can be the means of sinking both individual and church to the depths of despair. It is not to be wondered at that an all-wise God has stated in unmistakable language and defined in the clearest possible manner the uses and purposes of this extraordinary gift.

It has been openly taught in at least three different bodies of believers that prophecy was used in the early Church as a means of guidance to individuals and church. It has also been claimed that prophecy is still in the Church for this same purpose. The three bodies referred to are (1) The *Catholic Apostolic Church*, the outcome of the 1830 revival; (2) the *Apostolic Faith Church*, with headquarters at Winton, Bournemouth, which has come into existence since the present outpouring of the Spirit; (3) The *Apostolic Church*, with headquarters at Penygroes, South Wales, which was formed after a secession of its leaders from the *Apostolic Faith Church*. There are others of much less importance such as one called the *Apostolic Church of God*, whose official literature we also have before us. Nos. 2 and 3 believe in the establishment of an office of "*set prophet*," through whom messages of guidance can be given to their adherents. These messages through the "*set prophet*" are claimed to be the spoken word of God, and as such are infallible.

The practice in connection with this arrangement has come to be known as "*enquiring of the Lord.*" Further, the prophetical utterances of the "*set prophet*" practically control the affairs of their scattered churches. Through it, the "*spoken word*," apostles and all officers are appointed to office in the church.

To the *"spoken word"* members can look for guidance on questions of the most private nature relating to church, home, and business life. If any follower reveals the least uneasiness concerning the accuracy or wisdom of the message uttered, he is sometimes warned of fearful impending dangers. Implicit obedience is demanded, even though the instructions seem altogether foolish, for it is claimed that "the *Lord hath spoken.*" In addition to the *"set prophet"* there are subordinate prophets, but all prophecies of any importance must be submitted to the *"set prophet"* for confirmation, before any kind of action is contemplated. This, we believe, is a fairly accurate description of the system associated with the practice called *"enquiring of the Lord."* The Scriptures that are used to substantiate this claim will now be considered.

The Case For Enquiring Through Prophecy.

Now there were in the church that was at Antioch certain prophets and teachers; as Barnabas and Simeon that was called Niger, and Lucius of Cyrene, and Manaen, which had been brought up with Herod the tetrarch, and Saul. As they ministered to the Lord, and fasted, the Holy Ghost said, Separate Me Barnabas and Saul for the work whereunto I have called them. And when they had fasted and prayed, and laid their hands on them, they sent them away. Acts xiii.1-3.

The assertion.

The church at Antioch diligently enquired of the Lord through one who had the gift of prophecy concerning certain matters, including the appointment of church workers. While waiting upon Him, the Holy Ghost spoke through one of the prophets, saying, *"Separate me Barnabas and Saul for the work whereunto I have called them."*

The answer.

It does not say the Holy Ghost spoke through a prophet. It does say, *"the Holy Ghost said."* There were apostles, and teachers present in the church, as well as prophets, and the Holy Ghost might have given the message through a teacher. There is no mention of anything like the practice of *"enquiring of the Lord"* through a prophet in these verses. There are other scriptural examples of the Holy Ghost speaking when there is no prophet present. Surely the best commentary on the Scriptures is the Scripture itself. There is no mention of a prophet being with Philip in the desert of Gaza, yet the Spirit communicated a message to him.

And he arose and went: and, behold, a man of Ethiopia, an eunuch of great authority under Candace queen of the Ethiopians, who had the charge of all her treasure, and had come to Jerusalem for to worship, was returning, and sitting in his chariot read Esaias the prophet. Then the Spirit said unto Philip, Go near, and join thyself to this chariot. Acts viii.27-29.

Again, it does not say that the Holy Ghost spoke with an audible voice.

The Holy Spirit might have spoken through a prophet at Antioch, and He might have spoken with an audible voice, but it is wrong to insist that He did so when the Scripture is silent. It is positively dangerous to establish a practice of *"enquiring of the Lord"* through a prophet on what might have taken place at Antioch. There are other instances of the Spirit speaking, but we are not told how. If it is insisted that the Spirit spoke in an audible voice on this occasion the same must be said of the others. Surely God can speak to the innermost

soul, guide and direct, without doing so in an audible voice. No reasonable person would insist that an audible voice is meant in the following scripture:
And because ye are sons, God hath sent forth the Spirit of His Son into your hearts, crying, Abba, Father. Gal.iv.6.

The assertion.
There were prophets in Old Testament times who guided the people through their utterances.

The answer.
The pattern for Church government and its various offices is not in the Old Testament, but in the New. There are no indications in the New Testament that it is the function of prophets to guide the Church in the manner in which prophets guided Israel.

The assertion.
Agabus the prophet foretold things through the Spirit.
And in these days came prophets from Jerusalem unto Antioch. And there stood up one of them named Agabus, and signified by the Spirit that there should be great dearth throughout all the world: which came to pass in the days of Claudius Caesar. Acts xi.27,28.

The answer.
The foretelling aspect is really a very small part of the New Testament prophetic ministry. We do not dispute that God does occasionally reveal things that are unsought and unasked for through His children, as in the case with Agabus. But we do dispute the right to establish the
general practice of *"enquiring of"* or receiving messages for guidance through the gift of prophesy.

The assertion.
Agabus took Paul's girdle and prophesied.
And as we tarried there many days, there came down from

Judaea a certain prophet named Agabus. And when he was come unto us, he took Paul's girdle, and bound his own hands and feet, and said, Thus saith the Holy Ghost, So shall the Jews at Jerusalem bind the man that owneth this girdle, and shall deliver him into the hands of the Gentiles. Acts xxi.10,11.

The answer.

Here again there is no mention of "*enquiring of the Lord,*" and it does not say that Paul sought guidance from Agabus. There is not the slightest suggestion of such a practice in this incident.

The assertion.

The fact of there being "*set prophets*" in the Church.

And God hath set some in the church, first apostles, secondarily prophets, thirdly teachers, after that miracles, then gifts of healings, helps, governments, diversities of tongues. 1 Cor.xii.28.

The answer.

The absurdity of this title is very pronounced. If the liberty is given to convert verbs of the New Testament into adjectives for the purpose of providing handles to the nouns they govern then we shall be in a chaotic state indeed. We would have set apostles, set teachers, set miracles, set healings, set helps, set governments, set tongues. Yet this absurd proposition is put forth by men who claim to be leaders of the Church. It is either done in great ignorance, or with a wilful purpose to deceive their followers into accepting a most pernicious system of Church government. The New Testament never sets one prophet above the other in authority or power, and we certainly do not find that any are declared to be infallible. All utterances coming through prophets are subject to judgment on the part of the others, and to this plain rule there is no exception.

With regard to apostles, we believe that there is an essential difference between the twelve *"Apostles of the Lamb"* and the *"apostles of the churches."* The former were pre-eminently foundation Apostles whose names are fittingly inscribed in the foundations of the New Jerusalem. The latter were apostles strictly in the etymological term, for they were *"sent ones."* These *"sent ones"* or apostles are certainly in the Church to-day, and will be *"till we all come to the unity of the faith."* Besides these there were also false apostles in the early Church, as there are to-day, but they have different characteristics, among which self-importance and self-glorification are very prominent.

But what I do, that I will do, that I may cut off occasion from them which desire occasion; that wherein they glory, they may be found even as we. For such are false apostles, deceitful workers, transforming themselves into the apostles of Christ. 2Cor.xi.12,13.

The assertion.

Timothy was appointed to office.

Neglect not the gift that is in thee, which was given thee by prophecy, with the laying on of the hands of the presbytery. 1Tim.iv.14.

The answer.

There is no suggestion of Timothy being appointed to office in this scripture. It is not an office, but a spiritual gift that is in question, the neglect of which would impair Timothy's calling. The special gift within him that came by prophecy was an act of sovereignty by Him who has the prerogative at all times. It does not say that Timothy *"enquired of the Lord"* through a prophet, neither does it say that a prophet with an audible voice gave him a message. There is absolutely no basis here for the practice of appointing any man to office by prophecy, neither is there ground for setting up an unscriptural and therefore mischievous system whereby so-called infallible prophecies can rule the Church of God.

The policy of permitting the so-called "*set prophet*" to govern the Church has proved disastrous in the past, and enquiring of the prophet for the mind of the Lord on certain questions has led people into utter confusion. There is not a single scripture to show that it is the rule that the Lord's people should be guided by prophetic utterances. It is well-known to students of Church history that revival movements have been crippled by the obedience blindly rendered to the so-called "*word of prophecy.*" We shall consider one case in point that stands out as a danger signal to the great Pentecostal revival movement of the present day.

The Revival Of 1830.

This revival started in Scotland, and its spiritual phenomena caused an awakening in religious circles throughout the land! One of its features was the restoration of the miraculous gifts, which were very much in evidence. People baptised with the Holy Spirit were speaking in tongues and prophesying, while many miracles of healing were wrought in the Name of the Lord. Sometime after the commencement of the outpouring Edward Irving, minister of the *National Scottish Church* in London, identified himself with the revival, and it eventually resolved itself into the Catholic Apostolic Church. We shall have occasion again to refer to the signs and wonders that attended the revival, but at this juncture we shall only be concerned with the man,

Edward Irving, whose name loomed so largely with the movement. In the present-day revival with its signs and wonders we are continually reminded that this is another outbreak, only on a larger scale, of the *Irvingite* movement. This is mentioned with such sarcasm and contempt that the tendency among those who do not know is to conclude that Irving was a fanatic of the gravest kind. Therefore it would be well for us to have a glimpse of the man himself before judging his character. We are indebted to W. W. Andrews for the following in his writings on *"Edward Irving."*

"Suddenly, and to the amazement of everyone, in the spring of 1830, there was in the West of Scotland an outburst of supernatural manifestation in the form of tongues, and prophesyings, and gifts of healing. It was his faith in these as the work of the Holy Ghost, and in the restoration of the ancient ministries of the Church for which they prepared the way, that characterised the last few years of Mr. Irving's life, and led to conflicts, and
sufferings, and noble endurance, which gave a tragic interest to his history."

Testimonies Of Irving by some of his contemporaries are given in the preface to the second
edition of Andrews' work:

Carlyle.
"But for Irving I had never known what the communion of man with man means. He was the freest, brotherliest, bravest human soul mine ever came in contact with. I call him, on the whole, the best man I have ever (after trial enough) found in this world, or now hope to find." (Carlyle had been, from early youth, most intimate with him.) **De Quineey** (in *Literary Reminiscences*):
"He was unquestionably, by many, many degrees, the great-

est orator of our times... He was the only man of our times who realised one's idea of Paul's preaching at Athens, or defending himself before King Agrippa. An orator the most Demosthenic of our age."

Dr. Hamilton, Mr. Irving's successor in the Presbyterian Church, Regent Street:

"*Few have in these last times more marvellously united the pastor and the prophet, consecrated genius and assiduous affection, that intellectual sublimity which ennobles the topics which it touches... Seldom have bigger thoughts and loftier sentiments struggled for expression in human speech than those which are all but embodied in his magnificent orations... In his pulpit, as bold as the Baptist; he was in private, a very Barnabas, a son of consolation.*"

"**The North British Review,**" of August, 1862:

"*An intellect of great though somewhat unregulated power; a scholar of unusual attainments, at least for a Scottish minister; an orator whose amplitude of thought, and richness of imagery, and volume and flexibility of utterance, achieved some of the greatest triumphs of modern eloquence; above all, a man pure, true, brave, wholly genuine and Christian... In his moral character one cannot find anything mean or base, anything but what is true, pure and noble. He was not, as people once thought, puffed up with windy vanities, and the poor breath of popular applause... We see no trace of this poor craving in any part of his life. He was quite willing to become as nothing, if only the world would just believe with him... Verily and nobly, a true servant of God.*"

These expressions of opinion could be multiplied, but they are sufficient to show readers, who know little more of Irving than as of one whose name was early associated with a religious movement with tongues and prophecy in evidence, that he was, both intellectually and spiritually, a peer of the highest and noblest of his century.

This was the character of the man who threw himself unreservedly into the revival, won souls for the Kingdom, and established the Church amid conflicts and sufferings with unswerving faith. Edward Irving was a saint of God, loved and beloved of all, whose life burned upon the altar of service in the kingdom of Christ. Yet this saint of God erred in relying upon prophetic utterances for guidance. Even when charged with teaching wrong doctrine he pointed to the prophetesses who prophesied as the incontestable truth that he was right. The following kind but pathetic words of Mr. Andrews, the Congregational minister, who later "*took service under the Apostles as a Pastor,*" should sound as a warning note to all who participate in the great revival of to-day.

"*If ever he lost the poise and balance of his judgment, it was when he was brought into contact with this mighty outburst of supernatural utterance, which, with all his remarkable insight, he failed fully to comprehend, and to which, notwithstanding his great boldness and decision, and his firm vindication of authority, he yielded too unquestioning an obedience.*"

In his writings Mr. Andrews refers to failure of the prophetic utterance; he reveals that Apostles and Offices were appointed through prophecy just as so-called Apostolic churches do to-day. In fact that Church with which Edward Irving was associated, as regards its government, seems to be a replica of the so-called Apostolic bodies of the twentieth century.

Let those who are privileged to share in the present outpouring of the Spirit, and to witness the restoration of the miraculous gifts and offices, be determined that every gift and every office shall be controlled and guided by the written Word of God, and by nothing else. Those of us who have had occasion to attend services at any of the churches with which the name of Irving is linked have looked on at the gorgeous ritual and empty form, the grave-clothes of a once powerful church now in mourning, as a result of obeying too unquestioningly the word of the " prophet." If we are to be faithful ministers of the Word, if we are to be worthy leaders of the people, if we are to be sure guides in the Church's pathway, we must sound the warning note against the injurious practice of yielding implicit obedience to the so-called infallible utterances of a prophet.

Let us now carefully consider the possible sources of prophetic utterances. Messages From Three Possible Sources.

Most people are acquainted with two sources from which prophetic utterances can ensue, namely, *Divine* and *satanic*; but all are not informed of a third source, namely, the *psychic*, or *the human mind*.

It is from this source that messages which might cause contradiction and confusion can come. If this source is ignored by those who adhere to the unscriptural practice of *"enquiring of the Lord,"* or of taking guidance in any way from a *"set prophet,"* responsibility for disaster must be laid upon their own shoulders. Such an attitude means the paralysing of all reasoning faculties, and the abandonment of all righteous judgment. We are persuaded that if this matter was prayerfully and carefully weighed up in the light of the Scriptures and sanctified common sense, the practice would soon come to an end. Let us reflect on the possibilities of such a practice, bearing in mind that the so-called *"set prophets"* are human, and only possess the faculties of depraved human nature. How easy it would be for the mind to assert itself if the prophet is to decide by his utterance whether a person should sell out his assets and lay the proceeds at the feet of his brother Apostles. How easy it would be for his mind to express itself when calling out an Apostle or someone to a church office if the person called is a man of wealth or position. How easy it would be for the mind to dictate upon matters of importance when the gift is functioning, after the prophet has been sitting with the church officers, hearing and taking part in their discussions. Then again think of the possible confusion and disaster that could result from a possible mind-message. If the *"set prophet"* is to decide whether two should unite in marriage, and in doing so allow his mind to act, and the marriage with all its strained relations results in failure, the blame cannot be charged to God, but to those who foolishly acknowledge such a practice.

Again, messages from the mind can easily come through a *"set prophet,"* if he wishes to explain the reason why some particular prediction has not been fulfilled. The mind of the *"set prophet"* can easily assert itself in a prophecy that extols the privilege of a so-called *Apostolic Church*. The mind can easily come in to emphasise the benefits of the *"fuller vision"* in which its members are privileged to participate, in contradistinction to others less fortunate. The mind can certainly play a big part in these utterances when persuading their tithe-paying followers of some great and wonderful revival that is coming, which might prove to be as illusory as a mirage in the desert. To say that it is impossible for the mind to intrude in the utterance of the "*set prophet*" is tantamount to saying that he is not a free will agent, and is not subject to the common temptations of his fellow men. It is this psychical source that makes prophetic utterances fallible. If there were no such source we should only have to decide whether the messages were Divine or satanic, but as there is a third, namely, the mind, it must be taken into consideration.

We emphasise that any prophetic utterance can be interfered with from this third source, and those who willfully ignore this possibility are committing mental and moral suicide. More than ever we are persuaded that the only infallible Word is the written Word, and that there is no authority higher than the Bible. Therefore let all who are wise give heed to its inspired injunctions:

Let the prophets speak two or three, and let the other judge. 1Cor.xiv.29.

Quench not the Spirit. Despise not prophesyings. Prove all things; hold fast that which is good. 1Thess.v.19-21.

Prophecy: A Divine Boundary Line.

It has pleased God to fix a boundary line within which the gift of prophecy can operate. If it is confined to the prescribed limited sphere, it can cause both individuals and church to ascend to spiritual heights beyond the human comprehension. If it is allowed, as we have already shown, to break through the boundary line, the responsibility for extravagances and excrescences must rest on the shoulders of the transgressors. The Divine boundary line is raised within the covers of the

New Testament.
The Utility of Prophecy.
But he that prophesieth speaketh unto men to edification and exhortation and comfort. 1Cor.xiv.3.

```
            EXHORTATION
         /\
        /  \
       /    \
   EDIFICATION  PROPHECY
     /_____\
       COMFORT
```

If this gift were intended for the purpose of *"enquiring of the Lord"* through a prophet, with all that the practice entails, surely the objective of guidance would also have been named in this scripture. If it be argued that persons can be comforted and edified through an exhortation to be guided along special lines, our answer is, admittedly so, but there is nothing within this scriptural boundary line that admits of so-called infallible *"Set-Prophets"* or of a practice such as *"enquiring of the Lord,"* a system which experience shows can delude the children of God.

Prophecy Edifies The Church.
He that speaketh in an unknown tongue edifieth himself; but he that prophesieth edifieth the church. 1Cor.xiv.4.

Prophecy Used To Convict Unbelievers.
But if all prophesy, and there come in one that believeth not, or one unlearned, he is convinced of all, he is judged of all: And thus are the secrets of his heart made manifest; and so falling down on his face he will worship God, and report that God is in you of a truth. 1Cor.xiv.24,25.

The determined stand for this clearly defined boundary line will safeguard against all misleading and extravagant prophetical utterances. Within the confines of this scriptural line, the gift of prophecy is being exercised in thousands of churches to-day to the edification, exhortation, and comfort of the Church. If believers are in the need of guidance or help in deciding certain matters, let them pray, and afterwards consult older and more mature believers, who can give them the benefits of longer experience. Every prophetical utterance should be judged, and if there is the least suggestion of guidance in any prophecy, the persons concerned should feel intuitively within whether they ought to obey, and only contemplate action after consulting those who are in a position to judge without prejudice. Any vision that a person may have which indicates guidance should be dealt with in the same way. The believer who claims to receive instruction to act in any vision, should also bear in mind the Scriptural examples of guidance by vision, where God revealed His will to both parties concerned.

Ananias Knew: Paul Knew.

And there was a certain disciple at Damascus, named Ananias; and to him said the Lord in a vision, Ananias. And he said, Behold, I am here, Lord, And the Lord said unto him, Arise, and go into the street which is called Straight, and enquire in the house of Judas for one called Saul, of Tarsus: for, behold, he prayeth, and hath seen in a vision a man named Ananias coming in, and putting his hand on him, that he might receive his sight. Acts ix.10-12.

Cornelius Knew: Peter Knew.

He saw in a vision evidently about the ninth hour of the day an angel of God coming in to him, and saying unto him, Cornelius... And now send men to Joppa, and call for one Simon, whose surname is Peter. Now while Peter doubted in himself what this vision which he had seen should mean, behold, the men which were sent from Cornelius had made enquiry for Simon's house, and stood before the gate. Acts x.3,5,17.

The true pattern for the Church of Christ is in the New Testament, and in that pattern there is no room for any such system as *"enquiring of the Lord"*; **neither is there room for the setting up of an** *"infallible"* **prophetic office for guiding or controlling the Church.**

Chapter 13. Miraculous Gifts In Evidence Throughout The Present Age.

Testimony Of Church History.
While depending absolutely upon *"What saith the Scriptures?"* for evidence to prove that the days of miracles are not past, we do not recede from that stand by glancing into the records of Church historians. Concerning the baptism of the Spirit and miraculous gifts, there is indisputable evidence in Church records and memoirs of saints to prove the continuance of these after the days of the Apostles right down to the present day.

Eusebius' Ecclesiastical History. A.D. 98-117.
Speaking of the preaching evangelists that were yet living Eusebius says: *"Of those that flourished in these times, Quadratus is said to have been distinguished for his prophetical gifts. There were many others, also, noted in these times, who held rank in the apostolic succession... The Holy Spirit also wrought many wonders as yet through them, so that as soon as the gospel was heard, men in crowds voluntarily and eagerly embraced the true faith with their whole minds." Pages 111,112.*

A.D. 98-117.
Eusebius, from the writings of Papias, gives the following interesting account of poison being rendered harmless: *"Another wonderful event happened respecting Justus, surnamed Barsabas, who, though he drank a deadly poison, experienced nothing injurious, through the grace of the Lord." Page 114.*

A.D. 161-180.
These accounts are given by Irenæus in those five

books of his, to which he gave the title of *Refutation and Overthrow of False Doctrine*. In the second book of the same work, he shows that even down to his times, instances of Divine and miraculous power were remaining in some churches: "*Even among the brethren frequently in a case of necessity, when a whole church united in much fasting and prayer, the spirit has returned to the ex-animated body, and the man was granted to the prayers of the saints.*" And again, he says after other observations: "*But if they say that our Lord also did these things only in appearance, we shall refer them back to the prophetic declarations, and shall show from them that all those things were strictly foretold, and were done by Him, and that He alone is the Son of God. Wherefore, also, those that were truly His disciples, receiving grace from Him, in His name performed these things for the benefit of the rest of men, as everyone received the free gift from Him. Some, indeed, most certainly and truly cast out demons, so that frequently those persons themselves that were cleansed from wicked spirits, believed and were received into the Church. Others have the knowledge of things to come, as also visions and prophetic communications; others heal the sick by the imposition of hands, and restore them to health. And, moreover, as we said above, even the dead have been raised, and continued with us many years. And why should we say more? It is impossible to tell the number of the gifts which the church throughout the world received from God, and the deeds performed in the name of Jesus Christ, that was crucified under Pontius Pilate, and this too every day for the benefit of the heathen, without deceiving any, or exacting their money. For as she has received freely from God, she also freely ministers.*" In another place the same author writes: "As we hear many of *the brethren in the church who have prophetic gifts, and who speak in all tongues through the Spirit, and who also bring to light the secret things of men for their benefit, and who expound the mysteries of God."* These gifts of different kinds also continued with those that were worthy until the times mentioned. *Page 174.*

Historical Testimony.

The following testimonies, ranging from the fathers of the Early Church to the late revered Dr.

F. B. Meyer of our time, are taken from *With Signs Following*, so ably edited by our beloved brother, Stanley H. Frodsham.

Chrysostom.

Chrysostom, who lived during part of the fourth and fifth centuries, wrote: *"Whosoever was baptised in apostolic days, he straightway spake with tongues; for since on their coming over from idols, without any clear knowledge or training in the ancient Scriptures, they at once received the Spirit; not that they saw the Spirit, for He is invisible, but God's grace bestowed some sensible proof of His energy; and one straightway spake in the Persian language, another in the Roman, another in the Indian, another in some other tongue; and this made manifest to them that were without that it was the Spirit in the very person speaking. Wherefore the*

Apostle calls it 'the manifestation of the Spirit which is given to every man to profit withal.'"

Second Century.

Tertullian, who lived in the second century, speaks of the spiritual gifts, including the gift of tongues, as being still manifest among the Montanists to whom he belonged.

Fourth Century.

Augustine wrote in the fourth century, "*We still do what the apostles did when they laid hands on the Samaritans, and called down the Holy Spirit on them, in the laying on of hands. It is expected that converts should speak with new tongues.*"
Twelfth to Fifteenth Century.
Even in the Dark Ages God gave some gracious revivals. From the twelfth to the fifteenth century there were revivals in Southern Europe in which many spoke in other tongues.
Foremost among these revivalists were the Waldenses and Albigenses.
Thirteenth Century.
The Encyclopaedia Britannica states that the *glossolalia* (or speaking in tongues) "*recurs in Christian revivals of every age, e.g. among the mendicant friars of the thirteenth century, among the Jansenists and early Quakers, the persecuted Protestants of the Cevennes, and the Irvingites.*" 11th Edition, Vol. 27, pages 9 and 10. **A.D. 1419-1882.**
In the *History of the Christian Church*, by Philip Schaff, Vol. 1, page 237, of the edition of 1882, this author shows that the phenomenon of speaking in tongues reappeared from time to time in seasons of special religious revival, "*as among the Camisards and the prophets of the Cevennes in France, among the early Quakers and Methodists, the Readers (followers of Lasare) in Sweden in 1841-1843, in the Irish revivals of 1859, and especially in the 'Catholic Apostolic Church,' commonly called Irvingites, from 1831-1833, and even to this day.*" This church history says of Vincent Ferrar, who died in 1419: "*Spondamus and many others say, this saint was honoured with the gift of tongues.*" This work also tells of Francis Xavier, who died in 1552, that he "*is said to have*

made himself understood by the Hindus without knowing their language." The *Catholic Encyclopaedia* also speaks of him preaching in tongues unknown to him. Xavier was a truly converted man, and a most remarkable missionary.

A.D. 1685-1714.

Writing of the revivals among the Huguenots, Canon A. A. Boddy states: *"When Louis XIV of France in 1685 revoked the Edict of Nantes, which had given religious liberty, he strove by dragonnades to drive Protestants into the Roman Catholic Church. The Huguenots were led by John Cavalier, a farmer, into inaccessible mountains. Among the persecuted people were those who spoke in tongues. There are records both by enemies and by friends as to their prophetic gifts. Prophets came from the Cevennes to Holland, and on to Germany. At that time, among professors and students, there was great receptivity to God's power. In 1714 they brought the gift of tongues and prophecy to Wetterau, near Frankfurt-on-Main. Their leaders were an ejected Wurtemburg pastor, named Gruber, and a Brother Rock, a saddler. They and their 'gifted' followers were called 'the inspired ones of the Wetterau.'"*

A.D. 1750.

In the diary of Thomas Walsh, one of Wesley's foremost preachers, March 8, 1750, the record stands: *"This morning the Lord gave me language that I knew not of, raising my soul to Him in a wonderful manner."*

A.D. 1824-1909.

Mr. O. P. Simmons of Frost Proof, Fla., writing in *A Call to Faith* in November, 1909, states: *"While I have been a church member for sixty-two years, I have associated with those who talk in tongues for fifty-two years. In Southern New England, among the Second Adventists, A.D.*

1875, I learned that some had for three years previously in their religious worship spoken in what is termed as 'the unknown tongues.' From 1824 down to the present time, from Maine to Connecticut, quite a goodly number of the Adventist people (known as Gift Adventists) have had more or less talking in tongues, and also the interpretation of tongues.

Some gifted men of their ministry have been thus exercised. The most talking in tongues has been by Wm. H. Doughty, a minister for over forty years. He was the leader among the Gift Adventists. The writer knew him well. He was a very sweet-spirited, humble Christian, of great power in prayer. He was often called to lay hands on the sick, when some instant faith-healings of chronic diseases were the result."

A.D. 1885.

At an international conference held in England in 1885, Mrs. Michael Baxter, whose husband was the author of the well-known book, *Forty Future Wonders of Scripture Prophecy*, and the founder of the *Christian Herald* of London and the *Christian Herald* of New York, told of being able to preach for thirty-five minutes in German when she was almost entirely unfamiliar with the language. She was well understood and one soul was converted. She stated, "*After that He led me to speak almost every day, and often twice a day to hundreds of people, although when I went into a shop I could not make myself understood, nor could I understand the people.*"

Some years ago Dr. F. B. Meyer visited Esthonia, one of the Baltic provinces of Russia, where he found some simple peasant congregations of Baptists. He wrote to the London Christian of the wonderful work of the Holy Ghost that he saw among them. He stated,

"It is very remarkable, at a time when the Lutheran Church of this land has lost its evangelistic fervour, and is inclined to substitute forms and rites for the living power of Christ, that God raised up a devoted nobleman, Baron Uxhull, to preach the gospel in all its simplicity, and is renewing among the peasantry those marvellous manifestations which attended the first preaching of the gospel, when God bore witness to the message of salvation 'with signs and wonders and gifts of the Holy Ghost.' To have come across a movement like this is intensely interesting. The gift of tongues is heard quite often in the meetings, especially in the villages, but also in the towns. Here at Reval, the pastor of the Baptist church tells me that they often break out in his meetings. They are most often uttered by young women, less frequently by men. When they are interpreted they are found to mean, 'Jesus is coming soon; Jesus is near. Be ready; be not idle.' When they are heard, unbelievers who may be in the audience are greatly awed. A gentleman who was present on one occasion was deeply impressed by the fact that those who spoke were quite ordinary people, until they were uplifted as it were by a trance, and then they spoke with so much fluency and refinement."

One Of The Scots Worthies.

Among the worthy sons of Scotland whose record is included in *Scots Worthies* was one named John Welch. Endued with outstanding abilities, this saintly minister of the Gospel was a man of prayer. It is recorded that he would spend hours during the night in secret intercession on behalf of his beloved Scotland. He had endeared himself by his godly life and service to the hearts of the people amongst whom he ministered. This man's life and character has been held forth practically in every pulpit in Scotland as an example of saintliness, and of devoted abandonment to the cause of Christ. Yet in these references we understand that a strange silence is allowed to be drawn over that part of his life and ministry which was wrapped up in the supernatural. In our companion book, *Healing Rays*, we have devoted some space to show that in the name of his God even the dead were raised. We are now drawing your attention to a remarkable experience of his, in which if he did not speak in tongues, he manifested something very much like it, and also how he by the gift of discernment saved one whole town from a plague.

"As the duty wherein John Welch abounded and excelled most was prayer, so his greatest attainments fell that way. He used to say that he wondered how a Christian could lie in bed all night, and not rise to pray; and many times he rose, and many times he watched. One night he rose and went into the next room, where he stayed so long at secret prayer, that his wife, fearing he might catch cold, was constrained to rise and follow him, and, as she

hearkened, she heard him speak as by interrupted sentences, 'Lord, wilt Thou not grant me Scotland?' and, after a pause, 'Enough, Lord, enough.' She asked him afterwards what he meant by saying, 'Enough, Lord, enough.' He showed himself dissatisfied with her curiosity; but told her that he had been wrestling with the Lord for Scotland, and found there was a sad time at hand, but that the Lord would be gracious to a remnant. This was about the time when bishops first overspread the land, and corrupted the Church. This is more wonderful still: An honest minister, who was a parishioner of his for many a day, said that one night as Welch watched in his garden very late, and some friends were waiting upon him in his house, and wearying because of his long stay, one of them chanced to open a window toward the place where he walked, and saw clearly a strange light surround him, and heard him speak strange words about his spiritual joy.

"But though John Welch, on account of his holiness, abilities, and success, had acquired among his subdued people a very great respect, yet was he never in such admiration as after the great plague which raged in Scotland in his time. And one cause was this: The magistrates of Ayr, for as much as this town alone was free, and the country around infected, thought fit to guard the ports with sentinels and watchmen. One day two travelling merchants, each with a pack of cloth upon a horse, came to the town desiring entrance, that they might sell their goods, producing a pass from the magistrates of the town from whence they came, which was at that time sound and free. Notwithstanding all this, the sentinels stopped them till the magistrates were called, and when they came they would do nothing without their minister's advice; so John Welch was called, and his opinion asked. He demurred, and putting off his hat, with his eyes towards heaven for a pretty space, though he uttered no audible words, yet he continued in a praying posture, and after a little space told the magistrates that they would do well to discharge these travellers their town, affirming, with great asseveration, that the plague was in these packs. So the magistrates commanded them to be gone, and they went to Cumnock, a town twenty miles distant, and there sold their goods, which kindled such an inffection in that place, that the living were hardly able to bury their dead." page 124.

Rev. John Wesley On Miraculous Gifts.

The Rev. John Wesley, preacher, teacher, and reformer, whose name is treasured in the hearts of believers ever since the great revival of Methodism, can surely be considered a reliable judge as to whether the miraculous gifts should be in the Church today. The following is taken from his sermon on "*The More Excellent Way.*"

"*It does not appear that these extraordinary gifts of the Holy Ghost were common in the Church for more than two or three centuries. We seldom hear of them after that fatal period when the Emperor Constantine called himself a Christian, and from a vain imagination of promoting the Christian cause, thereby heaped riches and power and honour upon the Christians in general, but in particular upon Christian clergy. From this time they almost totally ceased; very few instances of the kind being found. The cause of this was not, as has been vulgarly supposed, because there is no more occasion for them: because all the world were become Christians. This is a miserable mistake, not a twentieth part of it was then nominally Christian. The real cause was: the love of many, almost all Christians, so-called, was waxed cold. The Christians had no more of the Spirit of Christ than the other heathens; The Son of Man when He came to examine His Church could hardly find faith upon earth. This was the real cause why the extraordinary gifts of the Holy Ghost were no longer to be found in the Christian Church : because the Christians were turned heathen again, and had only a dead form left.*"

Miraculous Gifts In 1830.

The following account of revival in 1830 is taken from the book *Edward Irving*, written by the late W. W. Andrews. The attention of this writer was drawn to the spiritual phenomena in Scotland and England in 1831. His careful examination of the revival led him to believe that the miraculous gifts were of God. He continued in the Congregational ministry until 1849, when he became closely associated with the movement.

"There were similar manifestations in the family of the McDonald's, living at Port Glasgow, on the opposite shore of the Clyde. 'They were distinguished,' says Mrs. Oliphant, 'like these two young Campbells, for a profound and saintly piety, which had marked them out from their neighbours, and attracted to them many friends out of their own condition. The leading members of this household were two brothers, according to all reports, men of the soberest steadfast life, quietly labouring at their business, and in no way likely to be the subjects of ecstatic emotion."

Early in the spring of 1830, one of the sisters who was very ill at the time, was suddenly lifted up in the Spirit and made to pass through very wonderful experiences, in which (to use her own language) she *"felt surrounded by the heavenly hosts, a multitude which no man could number, and heard them saying, 'Aleluia, for the Lord God Omnipotent reigneth.' ...No language can express the glorious things which were made to pass before me. I was constrained to cry for a speedy revelation of the glory, that all flesh might see it."* The family accounted for these remarkable experiences on the supposition that their sister was dying, knowing that holy persons have often had visions of God in the last moments of life. Nearly two months passed away without any unusual occurrence, when the following events took place as related by one of them:

"For several days my sister had been so unusually ill that I thought her dying. She had scarcely been able to have her bed made for a week. Mrs.-- and myself had been sitting quietly at the bedside, when the power of the Spirit came upon her. She said, *'There will be a mighty outpouring of the Spirit this day,'* and then broke forth in a most marvellous setting forth of the wonderful works of God; and, as if her own weakness had been altogether lost in the strength of the Holy Ghost, continued with little or no intermission for two or three hours, in mingled prayer, praise, and exhortation. At dinner time James and George came home as usual, whom she addressed at great length; concluding with a solemn prayer for James that he might at that time be endowed with the power of the Holy Ghost. Almost immediately James calmly said, *'I have got it.'* He walked to the window and stood a minute or two. I looked at him and almost trembled, there was such a change upon his whole countenance. He then with a step and manner of most indescribable majesty walked up to Margaret's bedside, and addressed her in those words of the twentieth Psalm, *'Arise, and stand upright.'* He repeated the words, took her by the hand, and she arose. We all sat down and took our dinner. After it, my brothers went to the building yard as usual, where James wrote to Miss Mary Campbell, commanding her in the Name of the Lord to arise. The next morning, after breakfast, James said, *'I am going to the quay to see if Miss Campbell is come across the water,'* at which we expressed our surprise, as he had said nothing to us of having written to her (and she was thought to be dying). She came as he expected, declaring herself perfectly whole.

"It is not strange that Mr. Irving should have heard with joy and with a predisposition to believe, of this receiving of the gifts of the Holy Ghost... But he did not act rashly, nor come to any hasty conclusion... nor did he himself go down to Scotland at all, but in the month of August, three gentlemen, one of them a member of his session, and the other two members of the Church of

England, spent several weeks at Port Glasgow, for the purpose of examining into the alleged manifestations.

An account of this visit was communicated by one of them (Mr. Cardale, a solicitor in London, belonging to Baptist Noel's congregation) to the *Morning Watch*, for December, 1830. It is valuable as the testimony of a sound and sober-minded man, whose professional pursuits fitted him to weigh evidence with discrimination and impartiality, and who was not acting at all under Mr. Irving's influence. He says: '*These persons, while uttering the unknown sounds, as also while speaking in the Spirit in their own language, have every appearance of being under supernatural direction. The manner and voice are (speaking generally) different from what they are at other times, and on ordinary occasions. This difference does not consist merely in the solemnity and fervour of manner (which they possess), but their whole deportment gives an impression, not to be conveyed in words, that their organs are in use by supernatural power. In addition to the outward appearances, their own declarations, as those of honest, pious, and sober folk, may with propriety be taken in evidence. They declare that their organs of speech are made use of by the Spirit of God; and that they utter that which is given to them, and not the expressions of their own conceptions, or their intentions.*'

Charles G. Finney's Experience.

It was a red-letter day in the history of the Christian Church when Charles G. Finney left his profession as a barrister-at-law to enter its regular ministry.

It is almost impossible to think of Finney apart from his life of prayer, his holy living, his passion for souls, his masterly expositions and his faith in the supernatural power of the Spirit. His *Systematic*

Theology, Lectures to Professing Christians, and *Revival Themes* are among the best in our heritage of religious literature. We are drawing your attention to what this saintly and scholarly servant of Christ experienced when he was baptised with the Holy Ghost. The following is taken from his autobiography, and the words marked in italics describe an experience exactly like that of speaking in unknown tongues.

"*I received a mighty baptism of the Holy Ghost. Without any expectation of it, without ever having the thought in my mind that there was such a thing for me, without any recollection that I had ever heard the thing mentioned by any person in the world, the Holy Spirit descended upon me in a manner that seemed to go through me, body and soul. I could feel the impression like a wave of electricity, going through and through me. Indeed it seemed to come in waves of liquid love; for I could not express it in any other way. It seemed like the very breath of God. I can recollect distinctly that it seemed to fan me like immense wings. No words can express the wonderful love that was shed abroad in my heart.* **I wept aloud with joy and love; and I do not know but I should say, I literally bellowed out the unutterable gushings of my heart**. *These waves came over me, and over me, one after the other, until I recollect I cried out, 'I shall die if these waves continue to pass over me.' I said, 'Lord, I cannot bear any more.' Yet I had no fear of death... Thus I continued till late at night. I received some sound repose. When I awoke in the morning the sun had risen, and was pouring a clear light into my room. Words cannot express the impression that this sunlight made on me. Instantly the baptism that I had received the night be-*

fore returned upon me in the same manner. I arose upon my knees in the bed and wept aloud with joy, and remained for some time too much overwhelmed with the baptism of the Spirit to do anything but pour out my soul to God."

Mrs. M. Baxter On Miraculous Gifts.

The Rev. Michael and Mrs. Baxter have both passed on to the reward of their labours. Mr. Baxter was founder of the *Christian Herald*, a paper which was intended to be the main support of the teaching of the signs of the times. Mrs. Baxter, a real mother in Israel, was beloved of all for her untiring devotion to the cause of Christ. Her attitude towards miraculous gifts was recorded in the Christian Herald of May 12th 1910:

"We can never be judges as to whether any of the gifts of the blessed Spirit can or cannot be dispensed with in His working. There are some who think and say that the Holy Ghost's working in the way of physical healing, or in the gift of tongues, is not needed in our day; and that His working in wisdom and knowledge alone is necessary.

Let God be the judge: He hath 'set the members everyone in the body as it hath pleased Him,' and it is the workman who must judge what tools His work requires; the Head must judge with what member He can carry out His purposes."

Chapter 14. Baptism In The Holy Spirit.

Opposite Views Considered

In this chapter we propose dealing with the critics of our teaching on the baptism in the Holy Spirit and miraculous gifts. Any important subject of a controversial nature calls for prayerful and careful examination from every possible angle. We teach that the baptism in the Spirit is the birthright of the believer, and can only be experienced subsequent to salvation. We also teach that we are living in the closing days of the dispensation of the Holy Ghost, and that the Lord's people all over the world are experiencing the miraculous gifts of the Spirit in answer to prayer. We have always contended that it is unfair on the part of any student of Scripture to be positive regarding any truth, unless he can rightly and effectively deal with opposing views.

The baptism in the Holy Spirit and the speaking in tongues are subjects of great importance, and whatever stand is taken concerning them will have far-reaching consequences. To summarise, let us say that either hundreds of thousands of believers who claim to be baptised in the Holy Spirit, and are speaking in other tongues, are hopelessly deceived, or else certain teachers are helplessly astray on these subjects. Therefore, it is imperative that the matter should have careful consideration, for the issues are far greater than merely taking sides with some doctrinal views of minor importance. For the purpose of elucidation, we set out each critical objection with a following answer.

Critic: The baptism of the Spirit is connected not with

our state as Christians, but with our standing, and is the occasion and means of the believer's incorporation into the mystical body of Christ. This is proved by the first reference to the baptism of the Spirit in the Church Epistles. *For by one Spirit are we all baptised into one body, whether we be Jews or Gentiles, whether we be bond or free. 1Cor.xii.13.*

Answer: There is a great difference between the baptism of a person into the Body of Christ, and the baptism of the same person in the Holy Spirit. The baptism in the Spirit is undoubtedly referred to in this scripture. In order fully to comprehend the meaning of this passage we shall have to compare scripture with scripture. There are at least four baptisms mentioned in the New Testament, and in each case the subject is baptised in an element, into (or unto) something else.

I.—In The Cloud Unto Moses.

Moreover, brethren, I would not that ye should be ignorant, how that all our fathers were under the cloud, and all passed through the sea; And were all baptised unto Moses in the cloud and in the sea. 1Cor.x.1,2.

This baptism in the cloud unto Moses cannot possibly mean that the fathers were actually baptised into Moses; it can only mean that they were baptised in the cloud because of their state as followers of Moses.

II.—In Water Unto Repentance.

I indeed baptise you with water unto repentance: but He that cometh after me is mightier than I, whose shoes I am not worthy to bear: He shall baptise you with the Holy Ghost, and with fire. Matt.iii.11.

This baptism cannot possibly mean that John actually baptised his followers into repentance; it can only mean that they were baptised in water because of their state as repentant sinners.

III.—In Water Into The Name Of The Trinity.

Go ye therefore, and teach all nations, baptising them in (lit: into) the name of the Father, and of the Son, and of the Holy Ghost. Matt.xxviii.19.

This baptism cannot possibly mean that the believers are actually immersed into the Name of the Trinity; it can only mean that they are baptised in water because of their state as believers in the Name.

IV.—In One Spirit Into One Body.

For by (lit: in) one Spirit are we all baptised into one body, whether we be Jews or Gentiles, whether we be bond or free; and have been all made to drink into one Spirit. 1 Cor.xii.13.

In the three former cases the word **into** clearly shows that the subjects were baptised in the different elements because of their previous state. It is the same in this fourth scripture: the believers were baptised in the Spirit because of their state as members of the Body of Christ. Believers are incorporated into the Body of Christ when they receive Christ as Saviour; they subsequently receive the baptism in the Holy Spirit because of their state as members of the Body. The Samaritans in Acts viii, had received Christ as Saviour and had been baptised in water, before they received the Holy Spirit. If they had not been baptised into the Body of Christ before they received the Holy Spirit, they would have been baptised in water as unbelievers. *See Chapter III.*

The Divine Agent at the baptism into the mystical Body of Christ is certainly the Holy Spirit, for He convicts of sin and regenerates. But the Divine Agent who baptises those who are already members of the Body is the Lord Jesus Christ—"*...Upon whom thou shalt see the*

Spirit descending, and remaining on Him, the same is He which baptiseth with the Holy Ghost." John i.33.

Critic: There are seven words which are employed to set forth the mission and ministry of the Holy Spirit in relation to believers. These are:

1. **The Baptism:** *Acts i.5.*
2. **The Indwelling:** *1 Cor.iii.16.*
3. **The Gift:** *Acts ii.38.*
4. **The Sealing:** *Eph.iv.30.*
5. **The Earnest:** *Eph.i.14.*
6. **The Anointing:** *2 Cor.i.21.*
7. **The Fullness:** *Eph.v.18.*

In order to prove the case for a baptism of the Spirit for every believer, it would be necessary to regard these seven words as being interchangeable, and indiscriminately used throughout the New Testament, which they are not.

Answer: To understand the significance and force of any one of these words, they should certainly be considered in the light of their context and systematic use. To know whether any of them are interchangeable can be decided by a very simple test. If, for instance, it can be proved that three of them are used to describe one and the same experience, then such three at least are interchangeable. This is the case as regards what was experienced on the day of Pentecost. The same experience is described as a baptism in Acts i.5, as a filling in Acts ii.4, as a gift in Acts x.17. *See Chapter III., page 30.*

Critic: If the baptism of the Spirit is something that a believer may be without, something for which he should ask, and wait, how is it, let me repeat, that there is not a single word to that effect in the twenty-one epistles of the New Testament? We are commanded to be filled with the Spirit, but never to be baptised with the Spirit. The Baptism and the Filling are opposite figures. By the Baptism we are in the Spirit; but by the filling, the Spirit is in us.

Answer: The injunction: *"Be filled with the Spirit,"* in the Ephesian Epistle is identical with the baptism in the Spirit, as we have already shown by these interchangeable terms. The disciples on the day of Pentecost were baptised and filled with the Spirit at the same time. It would be an easy thing to demonstrate that an open vessel can be immersed and filled at the same time.

Critic: Let me refer to the speaking in unknown tongues and other signs mentioned in the sixteenth chapter of Mark: *Go ye into all the world and preach the Gospel to the whole creation. He that believeth and is baptised shall be saved; and he that disbelieveth shall be condemned. And these signs shall accompany them that have believed; in My name shall they cast out demons, they shall speak with (new) tongues; they shall take up serpents, and if they drink any deadly thing, it shall in no wise hurt them; they shall lay hands on the sick, and they shall recover. Mark xvi.15-18.*

These signs of which our Lord spoke were evidential signs, given to confirm the gospel preached and believed during the days of the apostles, an age which was unique in character, in that it saw the end of the old economy and the beginning of the new. Once the purpose for which they were given was accomplished, they were withdrawn, and were no longer vouchsafed. We affirm therefore that present-day claims to the exercise of them are without Scripture warrant or proof.

Answer: The scope for the proclamation of the Gospel in Mark xvi, extends to the whole world and to every creature, without distinction of class. Every geographical boundary is entirely wiped out, so that the message is to be carried to the uttermost parts of the earth. The command to go and preach is to be obeyed until the message shall fall upon the ears of the last man on earth. If there are no limits as regards place, time, or class to the command, why should there be any limit to place, time, or class as regards the promise of the miraculous signs which are promised in confirmation? If the signs are limited the Gospel message is limited, for the scope of the promise extends to the scope of the command. There is not a single scripture to show that they should cease as long as the Gospel is proclaimed. This scripture definitely states that the signs shall follow them that believe, which church history confirms, and as long as there are believers there will be the signs, for no clearer statement could possibly be made.

Critic: It is a fact of momentous significance that all the references in the Acts of the Apostles to the baptism of the Spirit, and to the accompanying sign of tongues, belong to the transition period represented by chapters ii.-xii. The reference in xix. 1-6 is only an apparent exception, for when the Apostle Paul went to Ephesus, he did not make these disciples, but found them; they were, therefore, not his converts.

Answer: We have come across quite a number who have raised up dispensational walls in different parts of the Book of Acts, but they are built upon the moveable sands of supposition, and not on the solid rock of Scripture.

Neither is there any evidence in Scripture to prove that difference was made between converts of one apostle and those of another. The book of the Acts of the Apostles records the doings of the Lord's people at the commencement of the present dispensation. The inspired Book of the Canon of Scripture certainly came to a close, but the dispensation continued, and so did the Acts of the Holy Ghost.

Critic: The ability to speak in unknown tongues was not a gift; it was a sign; and there is a scriptural distinction between gifts and signs. The former are permanent, the latter are temporary. Now there is no reference to tongues as a gift in the Acts of the Apostles, which of course marks it as one of the signs that has served its purpose and gone.

Answer: The speaking with tongues that accompanied the disciples at Pentecost was a gift as well as a sign. This is conclusively proved by T. J. McCrossan, B.A., B.D., formerly teacher of Greek in Manitoba University: "Just here let us compare Acts ii.4 with Acts iv.31. Acts ii.4: *'And they were all filled [eplésthésan,* aorist tense or past completed action] *with the Holy Ghost, and they began to speak with other tongues as the Spirit gave [epidou,* imperfect tense, or continued and repeated action*] to them to utter forth."* Acts iv.31: *'And when they had prayed, the place was shaken where they were assembled together, and they were all filled [eplésthésan —* the same word and the same aorist tense as Acts ii. 4] *with the Holy Ghost, and they spake [elaloun,* imperfect tense of *laleo, 'I speak'—* continued or repeated action] *the Word of God with boldness."* Note, these persons in Acts iv. 31 were just as completely filled with the Holy Ghost as those in Acts ii. 4, for the very same Greek word and the very same aorist tense are used in both cases to designate the completed filling. However, when they were filled, those in Acts ii.4 *spoke in other tongues, and continued to do so, as the Spirit gave* [*elaloun*, imperfect tense] *to them to utter forth*; while those in Acts iv.31, after their completed baptism or filling, as brought out by the use of the aorist tense, *spoke* [*elaloun*, imperfect tense] *the Word of God, with boldness, and continued to do so*, as the imperfect tense in Greek always signifies continued or repeated past action. The saints of Acts ii.4 therefore most assuredly received the gift of tongues after their baptism; those of Acts iv.31 the gift of prophecy. With thousands of unsaved Jews present, who spoke different languages, we can readily see why God gave the gift of tongues at Pentecost."

Critic: We are living in a dispensation when the highest level of faith is that which believes without seeing. The saints at Corinth were craving for signs, and when these came they were not a mark of God's nearness, but of His distance. Speaking in tongues was a sign of the absence of spiritual life and of antagonism to it.

Answer: If the speaking in tongues is a sign of the absence of spiritual life in one case, it must be in all others. Then the disciples at Pentecost, including the mother of our Lord, who were magnifying God in tongues, revealed the lack of spiritual life. The household of Cornelius and the disciples at Ephesus must also have been in the same condition. Paul himself must have lived in the lowest realm of spiritual life, for he spoke in tongues more than all.

Paul Gives His Testimony.
I thank my God, I speak with tongues more than ye all. 1 Cor.xiv.18.

Paul Expresses A Desire.
I would that ye all spake with tongues, but rather that ye prophesied: for greater is he that prophesieth than he that speaketh with tongues, except he interpret, that the church may receive edifying. 1Cor.xiv.5.
Paul Sounds A Warning Note.
If any man think himself to be a prophet, or spiritual, let him acknowledge that the things that I write unto you are the commandments of the Lord. But if any man be ignorant, let him be ignorant. Wherefore^ brethren, covet to prophesy, and forbid not to speak with tongues. 1Cor.xiv.37-39.
It is true that there were backsliders in the church at Corinth, but has there ever been any local church without them? Many sins which backsliders committed at Corinth are covered up in churches to-day, and are never brought to light and dealt with according to the instructions of the Apostle. It should be borne in mind, too, that this was also the church for which Paul thanked God at the beginning of this epistle, a Church that was in the attitude of waiting for the coming of the Lord.

Critic: Speaking in tongues and other manifestations have much in common with the effects produced by hypnotism, mesmerism, spiritism, and the like, and there can be little doubt that they may be attributable largely to such forces.

Answer: It were a sad state of affairs, were this true. Happily, we know better. We have often been told that to know a person one must live with him. Thank God, we have lived and moved amongst Pentecostal people, and we know them by the fruit they bear. In our ministry we have seen thousands baptised with the Holy

Spirit, and we have heard them speak with tongues. Yet we have never known one real Christian who, having sought the Baptism for service in the kingdom of God, receive an evil spirit. See Luke xi. 13.

Critic: The teaching with which the baptism of the Spirit and the speaking in tongues are connected would make the Holy Spirit the consciousness of the Church, whereas the Spirit has come to make the Lord Jesus Christ our consciousness. Speaking of these supposed miraculous signs as a whole, they are physical rather than spiritual in nature.

Answer: We have come into contact with hundreds of thousands during our ministry who have received the baptism of the Holy Spirit and the gift of tongues, and our testimony is that no people love and adore the Lord Jesus Christ more than they. Even the thousands of young people, who characterise the great Pentecostal movement of to-day, have fallen in love with Christ to such a degree that their lives are laid upon the altar of service, many on the foreign mission field, in the extension of His glorious Kingdom. Love for Christ is best proved by obedience to His will, and there are no more obedient people to the will of God than those baptised with the Holy Spirit with signs following.

Critic: The present Pentecostal movement with its miracles and gifts encourages extravagances and abuses of all kinds. The leaders I know would disclaim any responsibility for these excrescences, but the movement is wider than its leaders.

Answer: History shows that every heaven-sent revival is *"wider than its leaders,"* and every revival, like the present one, has had its excrescences. They are unavoidable where the Spirit of God is mightily at work, for the enemy is ever near, and ready to hinder along counterfeit and other lines. Every real revival movement has had to contend with three relentless opposing forces— the world, the flesh, and the devil—and the marvel is that revivals like the present one have experienced so little extravagance and excrescence. In latter years the greatest and most continuous revival since the days of the apostles is in progress all over the world. Every tongue and nation seems to be coming under the copious showers of Latter Rain, and the miraculous signs and gifts are freely bestowed. In its soul-saving aspect, through which lives and homes are changed, there has been nothing to compare with it in history. Within latter years thousands of scriptural and well-organised churches have been formed and established which enjoy the exercise of the spiritual gifts. As for Christian gatherings and conventions of the movement in the British Isles, there is nothing to compare with them in the land for spirituality and numbers. If the numbers of believers who attend the many and great Pentecostal conventions held concurrently in our land to-day were registered, the critics would be staggered. Is it to be wondered at that this revival is like all others in history, and has to contend with some excrescences?

Critic: The Church needs revival and it is encouraging to know that an ever-increasing number of saints are realising the great need. The prayers of God's people are everywhere ascending, and when the revival comes, it will be with the full and indisputable sanction of Holy Scripture, and will be confirmed by the fruit of the Spirit, and not by physical manifestations.

Answer: The revival which the Church needs has arrived, and there will be no other. It is useless praying and working if one is not prepared to receive. If the present heavenly visitation with its extensive soul-saving, its exhortation to holiness of life, its uncompromising stand for the whole Bible, its unshaken fundamentalism, its manifestation of the fruit of the Spirit, its exercise of supernatural gifts, its signs and wonders, and its implicit obedience to the commandments of Christ, is not accepted as the answer to prayer for revival, we should like to know what would be. We see no other pattern for revival in the New Testament, and the church or leader who rejects this is rejecting the answer to their own prayers for revival.

Chapter 15. The Supernatural In The Local Church.

Spiritual Gifts under Control

The work of a pastor in charge of a church essentially differs from that of an evangelist who travels hither and thither as a pioneer. The special and privileged work of the evangelist is to move from place to place, ever and anon, diligently seeking those that are lost. The special work of the pastor is to remain in the local sheepfold, to shepherd those who have been found. The church life itself differs from campaign life, in that it has to do with the settling down of the converts to conform to the pattern of the New Testament. Of all the beautiful figures that are used to describe church life, that of a house seems to us to apply in the superlative. It immediately conveys the idea of home and family life into which the convert is introduced as a member. After all his wanderings in the old life he arrives at the home prepared by a loving Heavenly Father. The methods and practices of the evangelist in campaign life outside in the world must necessarily differ in some respects from those that are more adapted to the life in the local church.

The evangelist is to go forging ahead, firing the dynamic of the Gospel message in the quarries of sin in quest of building material for the house. Then the material is to be cleansed of disobedience in the waters of baptism, and polished off by the baptism of the Holy Spirit. We are persuaded that the evangelist should endeavour to see that these three stages follow in quick and immediate succession in true Early Church manner: "*Repent, and be baptised... and ye shall receive the gift of the Holy Ghost.*" The pastor in his special calling is to handle the material carefully and wisely, so that it may be put into its proper place according to the pattern.

Our purpose in this chapter is to deal with the home life of the church. We have in the course of our studies unmercifully destroyed all the things that are not in the pattern, and we should be able to build the things that have true foundations in the Scripture. Of course, there are some things in church life and church construction that are not mentioned in the New Testament, and we must be careful where we are to depend, more or less, upon the sanctified reasoning faculties and righteous judgment.

The first thing that needs mentioning is the difference between conducting:
The Worship Of The Church And An Evangelistic Meeting.

By the church service we mean the one outstanding service of the week, when believers gather around the table of their Lord. Here the saints are in communion, and the worship of the heart can be better expressed in deep worshipful hymns, rather than in the lighter and more lilting songs of the Gospel service. This feature was borne in upon us in the early stages of our ministry, and we have never found it necessary to change our views. Of course, we do not cut out lively tunes altogether, but they are the exception and not the rule. Then again there is not so much need for physical energy in the church meeting as there is in the Gospel service. In the church meeting one can afford to relax somewhat and find more time for tuning in to the Spirit. One need never be anxious about rushing a worshipping service. Our experience is that it is more profitable and more important for the heart to go out in deep adoration, than for the meeting to go with speed and energy. The tendency for those inexperienced is to count upon making everything go.

We are not depreciating the abandonment of body and soul to the energetic service of Christ, but rather emphasising the ideal feature in a church meeting, that of deep spiritual worship. If the ideal church meeting for the worship of Christ as Head of the Church were borne in mind, the same few would not rush in with their prayers Sunday after Sunday to the exclusion of others. The sisters of the assembly would also see that the brothers were given a more forward place than themselves, thus acknowledging in type the headship of the Church. The prayers of the worshippers, too, would direct the mind of the assembly to Christ. Better have short prayers of one or two sentences, in order to lead to the adoration of Him, than long prayers that lead nowhere.

The next question to consider is the place and utility of **Miraculous Gifts In The Church.**

Right through this chapter the reader will bear in mind that we are dealing with the local church and not with the universal Church.

Healing in the church.

The ideal and most scriptural way of ministry to the sick is by adhering strictly to the pattern clearly defined in the Epistles to the churches of the New Testament. Anointing with oil appears to be the proper method in church life.

Is any sick among you? let him call for the elders of

the church; and let them pray over him, anointing him with oil in the name of the Lord : and the prayer of faith shall save the sick, and the Lord shall raise him up; and if he have committed sins, they shall be forgiven him. James v.14,15.

Those who need healing should be given an opportunity of calling for the ministry in the church. The command and promise of signs in Mark xvi.15-20 applies more to evangelistic work when the message needs confirming. The Scripture in Mark makes manifest the love of God towards those who are out in the world. The evangelist is sent forth with the message to the outsider, and on the authority of these verses he lays hands on the sick, regardless of the particular person's faith or obedience, and the signs follow.

But in a comparatively short time the evangelist moves on, and the signs cease. But in the church, where the gift of healing is permanently set, the believer is clearly taught to comply with certain conditions if he expects to be healed. Unlike the outsider, he is in the home, he is a member of the family, and his Heavenly Father expects the child to render continual obedience to His Word. Sometimes this is not forthcoming, and, as Father, He has to chastise and permit the disobedient one to be afflicted. The purpose for which this special kind of affliction is allowed would be lost, if the child was granted healing without ceasing to be disobedient. If healing services are conducted on campaign lines outsiders may continually come to be prayed for and not be healed, for the simple reason that the gift of healing, set in the Church, should be administered along church lines, and not expected as a sign which seems to be given to confirm the evangelistic message.

Of course, in this again, the transition stage from campaign work to the permanent church work should be prayerfully decided with much wisdom. But it does seem as if the people should conform to the Church pattern when it is decided that the campaign aspect is over.

Obedience In The Divine Family.
It is the work of the Pastor regularly to emphasise obedience to all in the house.

Obedience towards water baptism.
And he commanded them to be baptised in the name of the Lord... Acts x.48.

Obedience towards the Lord's table.
And when He had given thanks, He brake it, and said, Take, eat: this is My body, which is broken for you : this do in remembrance of Me. After the same manner also He took the cup, when He had supped, saying, This cup is the new testament in My blood: this do ye, as oft as ye drink it, in remembrance of Me. For as often as ye eat this bread, and drink this cup, ye do shew the Lord's death till He come. 1Cor.xi.24-26.

Obedience towards the support of the home.
Bring ye all the tithes into the storehouse, that there may be meat in Mine house, and prove Me now herewith, saith the Lord of hosts, if I will not open you the windows of heaven, and pour you out a blessing, that there shall not be room enough to receive it. And I will rebuke the devourer for your sakes, and he shall not destroy the fruits of your ground; neither shall your vine cast her fruit before the time in the field, saith the Lord of hosts. Malachi iii.10,11.

Obedience towards one another.
Confess your faults one to another, and pray one for another, that ye may be healed. The effectual fervent prayer of a righteous man availeth much. James v.16.

Obedience towards other communities.
Seeing ye have purified your souls in obeying the truth through the Spirit unto unfeigned love of the brethren, see that ye love one another with a pure heart fervently. 1Pet.i.22.

Supernatural Gifts In The Church.
When we come to consider the use of miraculous gifts in the Church there are two scriptures standing out prominently in the Word:

(a) *Every manifestation of the Spirit is given to profit withal (1Cor.xii.7).*

(b) *Seek that ye may excel to the edifying of the Church (1Cor.xiv.12).*

Although the miraculous gifts are distributed by the Spirit to the members of the Church, they seem to be under the control of the individual, and he can either use them or misuse them. This is proved conclusively by the injunctions given in the Epistles. We are fully persuaded that in order to have a local church working along scriptural lines, those in authority should guide and control the exercise of the gifts to the edification of the Church. Concerning the gift of prophecy, which all are enjoined to covet, we find that it calls for judgment in its exercise. If this gift, that takes such a leading place among the others, needed judging, how much more other gifts such as tongues, interpretations, and discerning of spirits. "*Let the prophets speak two or three, and let the others judge*" (1Cor.xiv.29). This method of dealing with the exercise of miraculous gifts would lead the church along the clear line which runs in between two extremes. On the one hand there are those who set up the fictitious set prophet, in the system of "*enquiring of the Lord*"; on the other hand, there are those who are fearful as regards the exercise of the gifts, and cut them out altogether. Take for instance the need of an acknowledged interpreter in connection with the following injunction: *But if there be no interpreter, let him keep silence in the church; and let him speak to himself, and' to God. 1Cor.xiv.28.*

This verse undoubtedly proves the case for such an acknowledgment, and its observance would avoid the suspense of waiting for some interpreter who might or might not be present to translate. The idea of persons speaking in tongues, not knowing whether an interpreter is present, does not fit in with this scripture. Then again, we are convinced that only members of the local church should exercise the gifts in the assembly. This would guard against the loose-living person who is for ever and anon tramping from church to church to exercise his gifts.

The wise leader of any church would not allow a stranger to take his place as pastor or teacher without credentials: how much more so with these delicate gifts and their far-reaching results. Those in authority could acknowledge an interpreter for a certain period, and then change for another as they wisely see the need arising, just like a change of ministry which at times is profitable to all.

The gift of tongues.

The gift of tongues is chiefly for private use when the individual is shut in with God. Its use in public is undoubtedly restricted to the church meeting, as the shows, and it is not intended to be used in other public or evangelistic meetings.

If therefore the whole church be come together into one

place, and all speak with tongues, and there come in those who are unlearned, or unbelievers, will they not say that ye are mad? 1 Cor.xiv.23.

That little word *"if"* is sufficient to prove that the Apostle is controlling the use of this particular gift, in a meeting where it is the exception and not the rule for unbelievers to attend. Here again those in authority, whose duty it is to deal with these spiritual matters, should decide if any other than the breaking-of-bread service should be regarded as a church meeting. This would settle the question as to whether the gift of tongues with its companion gift of interpretation should be exercised in prayer, Bible-reading, or convention meetings. Circumstances vary so much in different places that no hard or fast rule can be laid down in this connection, but the wisdom of having a proper understanding in each place is obvious to all. The number of messages given in one meeting should be limited to three, not necessarily by the same person, for it is evident that three persons can give one message each:
If any man speak in an unknown tongue, let it be by two, or at the most by three, and that by course; and let one interpret. 1 Cor.xiv.27.

Some people claim the right to break out in tongues when the preacher is speaking, but there is no warrant for such practice in the scriptures. We have known cases where this has been done with injurious results. It does not mean that the hearer must interrupt the preacher simply because the Spirit is upon him. He might be anointed to hold on quietly in real faith while the Word is going forth, and thus assist to the advantage of all. Here is a golden rule for worship and service which, if observed, will bring blessing to the individual and the church: *"And whatsoever ye do, do it heartily, as to the Lord, and not unto men"* (Col.iii.23). If the time has come for you to preach, or listen, or pray, or sing, do it heartily, as to the Lord and not unto men. With regard to the speaking in tongues, only the unlearned will consider that the exercise of this gift is more inspired than any other ministry. It is a glorious gift, and when properly controlled can be the means of unspeakable blessing, in edification not only to the speaker, but also to the church.

The gift of prophecy.

A comparison of two verses in the fourteenth chapter of 1Corinthians will show that messages in prophecy are also restricted to a certain number in one meeting:
Let the prophets speak two or three, and let the others judge. 1Cor.xiv.29.
For ye may all prophesy one by one, that all may learn, and all may be comforted. 1Cor.xiv.31.
There is no contradiction here, for in the former scripture the Apostle is regulating the use of the gift in the one meeting, while in the latter scripture he is encouraging all to prophesy in the general sense. All may prophesy one by one, but two or three messages only are to be given in the one meeting. This gift, like any other gift, is distributed among sisters as well as the Brethren.
Every man praying or prophesying, having his head covered, dishonoureth his head. But every woman that prayeth or prophesieth with her head' uncovered, dishonoureth her head. 1Cor.xi.4,5.

The purpose for which prophecy is given is clearly stated in the following scripture: *But he that prophesieth speaketh unto men to edification, and exhortation, and com-*

fort. 1Cor.xiv.3.

The misuse of this gift is dealt with in the twelfth chapter of this book. The great controlling factor in the Church is love, and without it there can only be disorder in the use of miraculous gifts. Love is never satisfied unless it is allowed to sacrifice, and it will never edify itself at the expense of stumbling others. Love is ever ready to suffer want, in order that the need of others may be supplied. This is beautifully illustrated in the attitude of the Apostle in connection with the gift of tongues. He knew by experience the blessing that ensued to himself from the exercise of this gift, yet how lovingly he declares—

Yet in the church I had rather speak five words with my understanding, that by my voice I might teach others also, than ten thousand words in an unknown tongue. Brethren, be not children in understanding : howbeit in malice be ye children, but in understanding be men. 1Cor. Xiv.19,20.

Love is most essential in the use of miraculous gifts. One can easily understand why chapter xiii comes in between chapters xii and xiv in the Epistle to the Corinthians. Gifts are mentioned in chapters xii and xiv, but the chapter on love comes in between. There is not a single gift out of the nine that can safely be exercised without love, and there is some aspect of love in chapter xiii, that applies to every gift in the other chapters. After all, followers of Christ are not to be known by their gifts, but by their fruit. It is possible to manufacture the semblance of a gift, but you cannot manufacture real fruit—it must grow.

The following illustration will help us to see the power of God in three aspects of church life.

Latent Power.
    This is illustrated by the beautiful liner that is for some time laid up in dock. That prodigious oceanic palace, lying so quietly at the quayside, gives no indication of life or power. Yet there are forces within that can send her ploughing through the stormiest of seas with tremendous speed. It only needs the slightest adjustment to translate her slumbering dynamics into kinetic motion. Even so many a beautiful church is giving no indication of the power at her disposal. It is lying dormant within, all because proper adjustment has not been made in accordance with the clear declaration of God's Word. When this is done, revival breaks out and life manifests itself; spiritual dynamic forces are let loose, and the church is driven through even the raging seas of opposition, worldliness, and unbelief.

Controlled Power.
The great liner leaves her moorings, glides down the lough, and moves out into the boundless ocean beyond. She turns first in one direction, then another; she proceeds slowly or quickly, all at the direction of the controls on board. Every possible precaution is taken in case of emergency; the clear lines of the chart are carefully followed, for every movement is under control. She proves to be a blessing in every port where she makes harbour, and her gracefulness is admired by all.

    What a splendid illustration she furnishes for the church which experiences revival. Adjustments to the requirements of God's Word have been made, and the dynamic of the gospel within has begun to manifest itself in unmistakable fashion. She gracefully leaves the cramped condition of the traditional quayside, passes through the lough of formal religion, and moves out into the great ocean of humanity. Her quest for lost sinners is rewarded, and perishing souls are safely quartered on board. She brings life to the dying, healing to die oppressed, power to the faint, liberty to the captives, and blessing to mankind everywhere. What disaster there would be if those on board the big liner were to neglect the controls, and allow her to proceed anywhere and everywhere.

Uncontrolled Power.
But what if the boilers were filled, the fires kindled, and the dynamic powers released in action, without control of any kind? The great liner would soon pound herself to pieces right at the quayside. Who can possibly imagine the appalling disasters which would ensue if she were allowed to pass out into the great ocean uncontrolled? Alas! this is an illustration of what is allowed to happen occasionally in a church blessed with the dynamic of the gospel. Having adjusted herself to the requirements of Holy Scripture, revival has broken out—the Spirit descends, the miraculous gifts are in evidence, and everything is on the move. Then, to the consternation of wiser heads, the hands are taken off the proper controls, and the power and gifts are allowed to run uncontrolled. The New Testament pattern of church equilibrium is upset, and it is not long before undue emotionalism, accompanied by excessive psychic forces, come aboard, with the result that the church in due time is split into pieces. The once powerful spiritual liner has become a wreck upon the rocks of excrescences and extravagance, and the end means disaster to all. If she had been controlled, and allowed to run according to the clear lines indicated by the inspired Chart, she would have been a blessing to a

needy world. The genuineness of the dynamic cannot be questioned, for there was nothing wrong with it. The trouble was caused by not acknowledging the need of control so clearly revealed in the Scriptures. Those in charge discovered too late that there was no real bondage in scriptural control, and no real liberty in uncontrolled power.

Chapter 16. Conclusion.

Mark xvi: Questions and Answers

And He said unto them, Go ye into all the world, and preach the gospel to every creature. He that believeth and is baptised shall be saved; but he that believeth not shall be damned. And these signs shall follow them that believe; In My name shall they cast out devils; they shall speak with new tongues; they shall take up serpents; and if they drink any deadly thing, it shall not hurt them; they shall lay hands on the sick, and they shall recover.
Mark xvi.15-18.

More controversy has raged around this portion of Scripture than any other in the whole Bible. It has been assailed by opponents and deserted by its friends. It comes under the judgment of both higher and lower critics, and we are sorry to say that if it has suffered at all it is at the hands of the latter. The higher critic is known to us all, for he openly declares himself antagonistic to a complete and infallible Bible. It is with an air of condescension that some of these lower critics are compelled to admit the inspiration and genuineness of this portion of the Gospel of Mark.

Yet if they succeeded in eliminating it from the canon of Scripture they would have to account for the signs that followed the ministry of the Apostles. The lower critic, while declaring himself to be the evangelical and fundamental custodian of the whole Book, is seeking to cut out all that promises supernatural manifestations in the present age.

The Word Confirmed.
And they went forth, and preached everywhere, the Lord working with them, and confirming the Word with signs following. Amen. Mark xvi.20.

Before considering the miraculous signs that followed in the Acts of the Apostles, let us now view some of the results of the confirmed ministry upon those who were converted.

Note the marks of these Early Church converts.

Then they that gladly received his word were baptised: and the same day there were added unto them about three thousand souls. And they continued steadfastly in the apostles' doctrine and fellowship, and in breaking of bread, and in prayers. And fear came upon every soul: and many wonders and signs were done by the apostles. Acts ii.41-43,

- They gladly received the Word.
- They were immediately baptised.
- They contended for the Apostles' doctrine.
- They manifested love towards the brethren.
- They continually remembered their absent Lord. They loved the prayer meetings.
- They witnessed signs and wonders.

These characteristics, we are glad to testify, are stamped indelibly upon the tens of thousands of converts that are being won to Christ in the present Four-

square Gospel and Pentecostal revival.
The Five Miraculous Signs.
And these signs shall follow. Mark xvi.17.
Demons were cast out.
And it came to pass, as we went to prayer, a certain damsel possessed with a spirit of divination met us, which brought her masters much gain by soothsaying : the same followed Paul and us, and cried, saying, These men are the servants of the Most High God, which shew unto us the way of salvation. And this did she many days. But Paul, being grieved, turned and said to the spirit, I command thee in the name of Jesus Christ to come out of her. And he came out the same hour. Acts xvi.16-18.
Disciples spoke in new tongues.
And they were all filled with the Holy Ghost, and began to speak with other tongues, as the Spirit gave them utterance. Acts ii.4.
For they heard them speak with tongues, and magnify God... Acts x.46.
And when Paul had laid his hands upon them, the Holy Ghost came on them and they spake with tongues, and prophesied. Acts xix.6.
Serpents were taken up.
And' when Paul had gathered a bundle of sticks, and laid them on the fire, there came a viper out of the heat, and fastened on his hand. And when the barbarians saw the venomous beast hang on his hand, they said among themselves, No doubt this man is a murderer, whom, though he hath escaped the sea, yet vengeance suffereth not to live. And he shook off the beast into the fire, and felt no harm. Acts xxviii.3-5.
Poison rendered harmless.
Howbeit they looked when he should have swollen, or fallen

down dead suddenly: but after they had looked a great while, and saw no harm come to him, they changed their minds, and said that he was a god. Acts xxviii.6. **The sick were healed.**
And by the hands of the apostles were many signs and wonders wrought among the people... Acts v.12.
There came also a multitude out of the cities round about unto Jerusalem, bringing sick folks, and' them which were vexed with unclean spirits: and they were healed everyone. Acts v.16.
Thus the five miraculous signs mentioned by our Lord at the close of Mark's Gospel actually
confirmed the ministry of the Apostles right up to the end of the inspired record.

We now proceed to answer questions.

Question: If you claim that these signs are following the ministry of God's servants in the
Foursquare Gospel revival of to-day, why are the dead not raised?

Answer: Amongst the signs which we have considered, the raising of the dead is not included. Therefore we do not presume to add anything to what is written. God can use His children to raise the dead as He did in the case of John Welch *(see chapter xiii,)*; but we are not out to claim all that God can do, but what He has specifically promised to do according to His Word.

Question: Were these signs not withdrawn at the end of the Apostolic age?

Answer: There is no Scripture to show that they were withdrawn. On the contrary Scripture definitely affirms that they were to be in evidence as long as the Church of Christ is in existence and as long as the Gospel is proclaimed.

Now ye are the body of Christ, and members in particular. And God hath set some in the church, first apostles, secondarily prophets, thirdly teachers, after that miracles, then gifts of healings, helps, governments, diversities of tongues. 1Cor.xii.27,28.

Question: But are they necessary in an enlightened age like ours?

Answer: It is not for us to question the necessity for these miraculous signs, for there is no Scripture to show that they should cease in the present dispensation. Again the Scriptures teach that the world is becoming more darkened as the age proceeds, especially when nearing the return of Christ.

Now the Spirit speaketh expressly, that in the latter times some shall depart from the faith, giving heed to seducing spirits, and doctrines of devils. 1Tim.iv.1.

Immediately after the tribulation of those days shall the sun be darkened, and the moon shall not give her light, and the stars shall fall from heaven, and the powers of the heavens shall be shaken: and then shall appear the sign of the Son of Man in heaven: and then shall all the tribes of the earth mourn, and they shall see the Son of man coming in the clouds of heaven with power and great glory. Matt.xxiv.29,30.

Question: But are we not definitely told that the miraculous gift of tongues shall cease?
1Cor.xiii.8: *"Whether there be tongues, they shall cease."*

Answer: In this connection we had better read the whole verse.

Charity never faileth: but whether there be prophecies, they shall fail; whether there be tongues, they shall cease; whether there be knowledge, it shall vanish away. 1Cor.xiii.8.

Here we see three things which cannot be separated from one another, and they must stand or fall together: prophecies, tongues, and knowledge.

Tongues have ceased, then also Prophecies have failed, and Knowledge has vanished away. If— Knowledge has not vanished away, then Prophecies have not failed, and Tongues have not ceased.

Surely you are not prepared to admit that prophecies, which include Old Testament Scripture, have failed, and that we are living in a world without knowledge?

Question: But does it not say, *"Covet earnestly the best gifts?"* Love is a better gift than tongues, which is the least of all gifts, for it conies with interpretation at the end of the list of miraculous gifts.

Answer: Love is not a gift, it is the natural product of the True Vine, of which all believers are branches. The fact that the gift of tongues comes with interpretation as the last of the list does not prove that it is the least. This way of interpreting the Scriptures is not a sound method, for we have another list— Faith, Hope, Love. Love comes last, but it is the greatest.

Question: The miraculous gifts were necessary during the transition period until the canon of Scripture was completed. When this was accomplished they were done away with, according to 1Corinthians xiii.10: *"But when that which is perfect is come, then that which is in part shall be done away."* **Answer:** If by *"that which is in part"* you mean the miraculous gifts, why not include the Old Testament (for it was only a part of that which is perfect), and regard the Old Testament as well as the miraculous gifts as being done away with? The context clearly proves that the words, *"that which is perfect,"* have reference, not to the completion of the Bible, but to the coming- of Christ. *For now we see through a glass, darkly; but then face to face : now I know in part; but then shall I know even as also I am known. 1Cor.xiii.12.*

Question: Are not some supernatural manifestations unseemly?
Answer: It all depends upon the eyes through which they appear as such. There have been occasions in religion when scenes have been described as unseemly, apart from any supernatural effect upon the body. Take for instance the ordinary baptismal services held in Baptist churches. Often the method of procedure and the dripping wet garments of the candidates have called forth censure as unseemly, by those whose opinions are biased or opposed to the truth of water baptism. We make no apology for physical manifestations, for they take place in every revival of religion. The reason why the more violent manifestations occur is the result of resisting and not yielding to the power of the Spirit. This was undoubtedly the cause of the many striking prostrations that occurred in the great revivals of 1859 and 1904. In such visitations it is only reasonable to find some folk resisting the Spirit to the extent of violent bodily manifestations, even to absolute prostrations. The whole revival movement is not to be condemned because of these manifestations. Wise Spirit-filled leaders will not condemn, but endeavour to instruct the people more thoroughly in the working of the Spirit, in order to eliminate this kind.

Question: Are we not revealing a lack of faith by asking to see signs and wonders?

Answer: We have often emphasised that Christianity is a religion of signs and wonders from beginning to end. It is essentially a religion of the supernatural. Signs of regeneration are to be seen in the changed lives of its real converts. If the signs are not seen, the converts are not producing the evidence that they have exercised real faith in Christ. It is the real faith that produces the evidential signs.

Yea, a man may say, Thou hast faith, and I have works: shew me thy faith without thy works, and I will shew thee my faith by my works. James ii.18.

And by the hands of the apostles were many signs and wonders wrought among the people... Acts v.12.

And the word of God increased; and the number of the disciples multiplied in Jerusalem greatly; and a great company of the priests were obedient to the faith. And Stephen, full of faith and power, did great wonders and miracles among the people. Acts vi.7,8.

Question: Is there not a danger of someone receiving an evil spirit by waiting for a physical manifestation?

Answer: There can be no danger of any person receiving an evil spirit if he is seeking the baptism with the Holy Spirit, or if he is seeking the gift of the Spirit for the glory of Christ. *And I say unto you, Ask, and it shall be given you; seek, and ye shall find; knock, and it shall be opened unto you... If a son shall ask bread of any of you that is a father, will he give him a stone? or if he ask a fish, will he for a fish give him a serpent? Or if he shall ask an egg, will he offer him a scorpion? If ye then, being evil, know how to give good gifts unto your children: how much more shall your Heavenly Father give the Holy Spirit to them that ask Him? Luke xi.9-13.*

Question: Is there not a danger of people becoming emotional if they receive the Baptism?

Answer: God calls for the sanctification of spirit, soul, and body. The sanctification of the soul means the sanctification of the emotions, for you cannot sever one from the other. The subtle arch-enemy of souls is exceedingly clever in teaching some Christians to stifle all emotion in the service of Christ. He knows that there can be no real revival of religion as long as they follow out his instructions. We are reminded of the words of Professor Henry Drummond in this connection: "*We learn from Peter's recovery that spiritual experience is intense. Peter wept bitterly. And this short sentence for ever settles the question of emotion in religion. The man who gives himself to earnest thought upon his ways will always have enough emotion to generate religious fervour in his soul.*"

We now conclude our studies on the baptism and gifts of the Holy Spirit, praying that our readers, if they have not yet received their birthright as believers, may believe and receive it for the glory of our Lord.

PRINCIPAL GEORGE JEFFREYS
Founder and Leader
of the
Elim Foursquare Gospel Alliance.

GEORGE JEFFREYS

PENTECOSTAL RAYS

Top: The Principal in the Queen's Hall, London.

Foursquare Gospellers packed the hall from floor to roof. Bottom: Principal George Jeffreys baptising in his College Grounds, London. Foursquare Gospellers following their Lord through the waters of baptism.

List Of Illustrations
Frontispiece
Royal Albert Hall, London......
The Crystal Palace, London The Queen's Hall, London ... The Elim Bible College, London The Usher Hall, Edinburgh The Ulster Hall, Belfast   The Cory Hall, Cardiff ...... The Bingley Hall, Birmingham ...

---

[1] The reader should be aware that this distinction is not Biblical. I

believe Jeffreys was intending to differentiate between regeneration and Spirit baptism (a valid distinction) but by focusing on two different titles of the Holy Spirit he has made an erroneous statement.

Printed in Great Britain
by Amazon